EASY CHINESE
易捷汉语

Speak Out Ⅰ
实用会话 上

主　编：邵力敏　刘　彤
编　者：梁德惠　杨　茵　鞠海钰

图书在版编目（CIP）数据

易捷汉语·实用会话：精装版.上册 / 邵力敏，刘彤主编. —2版.
—北京：北京语言大学出版社，2011.1
ISBN 978-7-5619-2959-9

Ⅰ.①易… Ⅱ.①邵… ②刘… Ⅲ.①汉语－口语－对外汉语教学
－教材 Ⅳ.①H195.4

中国版本图书馆CIP数据核字（2010）第258492号

易捷汉语·实用会话（上册）

责任编辑：冯　倩
责任印制：陈　辉

出版发行：**北京语言大学出版社**
社　　址：北京市海淀区学院路15号　　邮政编码：100083
网　　址：www.blcup.com
电　　话：发行部 82303650 / 3591 / 3648
　　　　　编辑部 82301016
　　　　　读者服务部 82303653 / 3908
　　　　　网上订购电话 82303668
　　　　　客户服务信箱 service@blcup.net
印　　刷：北京中科印刷有限公司
经　　销：全国新华书店

版　　次：2011年3月第2版　2011年3月第1次印刷
开　　本：850毫米×1168毫米　1/32　印张：4.75
字　　数：153千字　　印数：1-1000册
书　　号：ISBN 978-7-5619-2959-9/H·10345
定　　价：88.00元（含MP3和DVD）

凡有印装质量问题，本社负责调换。电话：82303590

前　言

　　易捷汉语系列教材是专门为非在校学习者编写的。名为"易捷",标示着这个系列教材的特点:实用易学,快捷速成。它的目的是让更多的人都有机会接触汉语,可以不去学校、可以没有老师、可以不用整块的时间,可以不管令人头痛的语法规则和笔画复杂的汉字,在短时间里会说一些汉语、认识一些有用的汉字,并且可以用学到的东西跟中国朋友交流或者应付一点儿实际问题。

　　易捷汉语系列教材包括两部:《轻松入门》适用于那些对汉语和中国文化感兴趣,想了解中国文化并想学一点儿基本交际汉语的外国朋友;《实用会话》适用于那些没有很多时间学习,但在工作或生活中又很需要用一些基本的汉语来应付工作或生活的外国朋友。

　　易捷汉语系列教材不仅可以做学习汉语的教材,还可以用作在中国生活、学习、工作、旅行时的应急汉语指南。

　　易捷汉语系列教材有图书、录音MP3、情景DVD等多种媒体互相配套,还可以通过电视网络和互联网传播,它是一个多种媒体、立体化的对外汉语教材系列,为学习者提供了多种媒体和多种学习方式的选择。

主编

Preface

Easy Chinese Series is intended for learners not studying in school. In the title of this product, the word "Easy" says it all: this is an easy and practical Chinese course helping learners to get achievement fast. It is produced in order to bring more people into contact with Chinese, and to give them an opportunity to speak Chinese, write characters, learn to communicate with Chinese people and cope with some practical problems in a short period of time without going to class, having no teachers, nor grueling schedules, nor the drudgery of learning grammatical rules and writing characters with complex strokes.

Easy Chinese Series contains two parts: *Understanding Chinese* is produced for non-Chinese who are interested in Chinese and Chinese culture, and wish to communicate with Chinese people. *Speak Out* is produced for learners who have little time, but have to use basic Chinese in their daily work or life.

Easy Chinese Series can be used not only as study material, but also as an emergency reference while living, studying, working or traveling in China.

Easy Chinese Series is a multimedia set including books, MP3s and DVDs. It can also be used via television networks or the Internet. It offers learners a multimedia, multi-faceted option for learning Chinese.

Chief Compiler

编写说明

《易捷汉语——实用会话》是为学过3~6个月汉语、有语音基础、掌握一定量词汇的汉语学习者而编写、制作的。它突出语言学习的实用性，旨在使学习者熟悉中国的实际生活环境，帮助学习者提高实际生活中的汉语会话能力，更快地适应汉语地区的生活和工作。教材中的会话场景涵盖了外国人在中国可能遇到的各种情形，如吃饭、购物、旅游、访友、洗衣、问路等；同时还引进了许多当代社会生活内容，如寄EMS（特快专递）、上网、唱卡拉OK等。

《易捷汉语——实用会话》分上、下两册，共四十课，每课包括以下六个部分：

▶ 你知道吗？（Do You Know?）：介绍本课所涉及场景的相关背景知识，了解这些，有助于你遇到类似场合的时候知道自己该怎么做。

▶ 生词（Vocabulary）：给出本课的关键词语，弄懂了这些词语，进入后面的学习时，你就不会感到困难了。

▶ 句型（Sentence Patterns）：列出本课主要用到的句型，可以给你的学习起个提示作用。

▶ 情景会话（Situational Conversations）：通过这里的会话，你可以看到在某些场合下，实际生活中人们是怎么用汉语来表达的。

▶ 常用表达法（Useful Phrases and Expressions）：对本课中出现的常用表达句型给以讲解，并不是复杂的语法讲解，主要是告诉你这个表达可以怎么用，用在什么地方。

▶ 练习（Exercises）：练习的方式主要有三种。

- "读一读"的词语你可以记住，并且可以用到你已经学会的句型中进行替换；

- "试一试"是替换练习，你可以模仿着做，然后还可以从"读一读"中找到合适的词语进行扩充；

- "能力训练"会给你几个情景，你可以试试把这课学过的所有词语和句型都用上，用汉语去应付这些场合，如果你能流利自如地表达，那说明这课内容你已经都掌握了。

使用这部教材，你不必担心认汉字困难的问题。无论在书里还是在DVD里，生词、会话等学习内容和练习里的句子全都配有汉语拼音。借助拼音，即使你不认识汉字，同样可以学习并掌握口语。

书中某些标题旁边有耳机标志 🎧，表示这部分内容有录音。在录音MP3中，既有慢速的发音，为你展示清晰的汉语发音；又有正常语速的发音，为你展示中国人正常交际时的发音状况。某些标题旁边有光盘标志 💿，表示这部分内容有录像，你可以观看DVD中的影像，看看中国人在实际生活中是怎么表达的。

实际上，你不仅可以把《易捷汉语——实用会话》当做汉语教材来学习，还可以把它当成在中国生活、学习、工作、旅行时的应急汉语指南。把书带在身上，遇到需要的场合，即使还说不出来，也可以把书上相应的内容指给别人看，从而达到你的目的。

我们希望，将要来中国或已经来到中国的你，无论是来工作、来学习还是来旅游，《易捷汉语——实用会话》都能对你有所帮助，使你在中国一切顺利。

编者

To the Learner

Speak Out is for students with 3~6 months of Chinese learning experience, who have a basic understanding of Chinese and have already grasped a certain amount of vocabulary. It is practical in Chinese language learning, acquainting students with the Chinese cultural environment, helping them improve their ability to conduct daily dialogues, and allowing them to quickly adjust to life and work in various parts of China. The scenes of the dialogues cover a number of situations that foreigners may encounter when in China, for example: dining, shopping, traveling, visiting friends, washing clothes, asking for directions, etc. At the same time they touch on many facets of modern life in China, such as mailing express packages, using the Internet, singing Karaoke, etc.

Speak Out is divided into two volumes with 40 lessons altogether. Each lesson consists of:

▶ Do You Know? This part introduces the background information necessary for understanding each lesson, and for helping you learn what to do in similar situations.

▶ Vocabulary This part lists the key words of each lesson. Understanding these words will allow you to progress easily through the remaining lessons.

▶ Sentence Patterns This part lists the important sentence structures introduced in the lesson.

▶ **Situational Conversations** By studying these example dialogues, you can see how phrases and expressions are used in real life.

▶ **Useful Phrases and Expressions** Providing a basic explanation of the useful phrases and expressions in each lesson, this part tells you how to use them without getting into lengthy or complicated discussions on grammar.

▶ **Exercises** Exercises are arranged into three main types:

- "Read the following words and phrases", which helps you memorize the words and phrases and use them with the sentence patterns you have learned.

- "Substitution drills", which is to help you familiarize with the usage of words and phrases from 'Read the following words and phrases' by doing substitution exercise.

- "Practice your Chinese", which allows you to practice the vocabulary and grammar learned in that lesson based on the given situations. If you can fluently use Chinese to communicate in these situations, it means you have mastered that lesson.

While using these materials, you don't need to worry about the difficulty in Chinese characters. In the book as well as in the DVD, all vocabulary, exercises and dialogues are written in both characters and *pinyin*, allowing you to study characters while practicing your speaking ability.

The headphone sign 🎧 in the book indicates that there are corresponding recordings in the MP3, where the phrases, sentences and dialogues are read in both a slow speed and a standard speed. The slow-speed reading allows you to clearly hear what is being said and to focus on the proper pronunciation of each word. The standard-speed reading mimics real-life conversations, thus making it a practical real-life learning experience. In addition, the CD sign 💿 indicates that there are corresponding kinescopes for the dialogues. Learners can watch the video clips in the DVD that depict real-life situations presented in the textbook.

Actually, you needn't only use *Speak Out* as a study aid; it can also be used as an emergency reference while living, studying, working and traveling in China. Take the book with you, and whenever you find yourself unable to speak the words you need, simply show others the appropriate part of the book to reach your goals.

We hope that *Speak Out* will be of use to you regardless of whether you will or have already come to work, study or travel in China, and always smooth your way during your stay in China.

Compilers

目 录

词类缩写表　　　　　　　　　　　　　　　　　1
Cílèi Suōxiě Biǎo
Abbreviations for Parts of Speech

第一课　　　　　入关检查　　　　　　　　　　2
Dì-yī Kè　　　　Rù Guān Jiǎnchá
Lesson 1　　 Going through the Customs

第二课　　　　　取行李　　　　　　　　　　　8
Dì-èr Kè　　　　Qǔ Xíngli
Lesson 2　　 Claiming Luggage

第三课　　　　　找洗手间　　　　　　　　　　14
Dì-sān Kè　　　Zhǎo Xǐshǒujiān
Lesson 3　　 Looking for a Washroom

第四课　　　　　坐出租车　　　　　　　　　　20
Dì-sì Kè　　　　Zuò Chūzūchē
Lesson 4　　 Taking a Taxi

第五课　　　　　换钱　　　　　　　　　　　　26
Dì-wǔ Kè　　　 Huàn Qián
Lesson 5　　 Changing Money

第六课　　　　　天气　　　　　　　　　　　　32
Dì-liù Kè　　　　Tiānqì
Lesson 6　　 Climate and Weather

第七课 Dì-qī Kè **Lesson 7**	预订房间 Yùdìng Fángjiān Reserving a Room	39
第八课 Dì-bā Kè **Lesson 8**	酒店登记 Jiǔdiàn Dēngjì Checking in at a Hotel	46
第九课 Dì-jiǔ Kè **Lesson 9**	换房与报修 Huàn Fáng Yǔ Bàoxiū Changing Rooms and Reporting a Repair	52
第十课 Dì-shí Kè **Lesson 10**	打电话 Dǎ Diànhuà Making a Telephone Call	58
第十一课 Dì-shíyī Kè **Lesson 11**	留言 Liú Yán Leaving a Message	65
第十二课 Dì-shí'èr Kè **Lesson 12**	找人 Zhǎo Rén Visiting Someone	71
第十三课 Dì-shísān Kè **Lesson 13**	洗衣 Xǐ Yī Doing Laundry	78
第十四课 Dì-shísì Kè **Lesson 14**	结账 Jié Zhàng Paying the Bill	85

第十五课　　　　问路　　　　　　　　　　　92
Dì-shíwǔ Kè　　Wèn Lù
Lesson 15　　Asking for Directions

第十六课　　　　乘车　　　　　　　　　　　99
Dì-shíliù Kè　　Chéng Chē
Lesson 16　　Means of Transportation

第十七课　　　　发传真与寄快递　　　　　　106
Dì-shíqī Kè　　Fā Chuánzhēn Yǔ Jì Kuàidì
Lesson 17　　Sending a Fax or an Express Mail

第十八课　　　　在邮局　　　　　　　　　　113
Dì-shíbā Kè　　Zài Yóujú
Lesson 18　　At a Post Office

第十九课　　　　点菜 I　　　　　　　　　　120
Dì-shíjiǔ Kè　　Diǎn Cài I
Lesson 19　　Ordering Dishes (I)

第二十课　　　　点菜 II　　　　　　　　　　127
Dì-èrshí Kè　　Diǎn Cài II
Lesson 20　　Ordering Dishes (II)

词语索引　　　　　　　　　　　　　　　　　134
Cíyǔ Suǒyǐn
Index of Words and Phrases

词类缩写表
Abbreviations for Parts of Speech

Abbreviation	Grammar Terms in English	Grammar Terms in Chinese
adj.	Adjective	形容词
adv.	Adverb	副词
ap.	Adjective Phrase	形容词短语
IE.	Idiomatic Expression	习惯用语
int.	Interjection	叹词
m.	Measure Word	量词
mdpt.	Modal Particle	语气助词
n.	Noun	名词
np.	Noun Phrase	名词短语
num.	Numerals	数词
opv.	Optative Verb	能愿动词
part.	Particle	助词
pn.	Proper Noun	专有名词
pre.	Prefix	词头
prep.	Preposition	介词
pron.	Pronoun	代词
qp.	Question Pronoun	疑问代词
v.	Verb	动词
vp.	Verb Phrase	动词短语

入关检查
Rù Guān Jiǎnchá
Going through the Customs

你知道吗?
Do you know?

When entering or leaving China, every passenger needs to hold a passport and a valid entry or exit visa for the customs to check. Normally, an incoming passenger will be required to fill in a landing card before landing, which includes such items as name, date of entry, purpose of trip, flight number, etc. The card is written in both Chinese and English, saving trouble for those who can not read Chinese. Similarly, an outgoing passenger shall present to the customs a departure card and a customs declaration, providing such information as name, birth date, purpose of trip, date of departure, flight number, etc.

Going through the Customs

生词 Vocabulary

❶	生意	shēngyi	n.	business
❷	海关	hǎiguān	n.	customs
❸	入境	rù jìng	v.	enter the customs
❹	手续	shǒuxù	n.	procedures; formalities
❺	护照	hùzhào	n.	passport

句型 Sentence Patterns

❶ 我来中国……
  Wǒ lái Zhōngguó ……

❷ 这是……
  Zhè shì ……

情景会话 Situational Conversations

I

[Two passengers are just getting off the plane, and they are talking.]

旅客甲：你来中国做什么？
　　　　Nǐ lái Zhōngguó zuò shénme?
　　　　Why have you come to China?

旅客乙：我来学汉语。你呢？
Wǒ lái xué Hànyǔ. Nǐ ne?
I've come to learn Chinese. How about you?

旅客甲：我来中国做生意。
Wǒ lái Zhōngguó zuò shēngyi.
I've come to China to do business.

II

[They are waiting to get through the procedures of the customs.]

旅客甲：办海关入境手续的时候，他们要看你的机票和护照。
Bàn hǎiguān rù jìng shǒuxù de shíhou, tāmen yào kàn nǐ de jīpiào hé hùzhào.
When you go through immigration and customs, they will ask to see your airline ticket and passport.

旅客乙：没问题。这是我的机票和护照。
Méi wèntí. Zhè shì wǒ de jīpiào hé hùzhào.
No problem. Here are my airline ticket and passport.

常用表达法
Useful Phrases and Expressions

1. 我来中国学汉语。
Wǒ lái Zhōngguó xué Hànyǔ.
I've come to China to learn Chinese.

If you are asked by someone why you've come to China, you can say: "Wǒ lái Zhōngguó……" The following are more examples:

Going through the Customs

❶ 我来中国做生意。
Wǒ lái Zhōngguó zuò shēngyi.
I've come to China to do business.

❷ 我来中国看朋友。
Wǒ lái Zhōngguó kàn péngyou.
I've come to China to visit a friend.

2. 这是我的机票和护照。
Zhè shì wǒ de jīpiào hé hùzhào.
Here are my airline ticket and passport.

When customs officials are checking your papers and personal belongings, you can say: "Zhè shì……" Here are more examples:

❶ 这是我的照相机。
Zhè shì wǒ de zhàoxiàngjī.
This is my camera.

❷ 这是我给朋友的礼物。
Zhè shì wǒ gěi péngyou de lǐwù.
This is a gift for my friend./These are gifts for my friends.

练习
Exercises

一、读一读 Read the following words and phrases.

上大学	shàng dàxué	go to college
看朋友	kàn péngyou	visit friends
看亲戚	kàn qīnqi	visit relatives
旅游	lǚyóu	travel
工作	gōngzuò	work

做生意	zuò shēngyi	do business
买东西	mǎi dōngxi	buy something
手机	shǒujī	cell phone
电脑	diànnǎo	computer
照相机	zhàoxiàngjī	camera
海关申报单	hǎiguān shēnbàodān	customs declaration
健康申报单	jiànkāng shēnbàodān	health declaration
入境登记卡	rùjìng dēngjìkǎ	landing card
出境登记卡	chūjìng dēngjìkǎ	departure card

二、试一试 Substitution drills.

1. ——你来中国做什么？
   Nǐ lái Zhōngguó zuò shénme?

   ——我来中国<u>学汉语</u>。
   Wǒ lái Zhōngguó xué Hànyǔ.

> 工作
> gōngzuò
>
> 买东西
> mǎi dōngxi
>
> 上大学
> shàng dàxué
>
> 看朋友
> kàn péngyou
>
> 旅游
> lǚyóu

2. 这是我的**机票**和**护照**。
   Zhè shì wǒ de **jīpiào** hé **hùzhào**.

> 电脑
> diànnǎo
>
> 海关申报单
> hǎiguān shēnbàodān
>
> 手机
> shǒujī
>
> 东西
> dōngxi
>
> 健康申报单
> jiànkāng shēnbàodān

三、能力训练 Practice your Chinese.

1. 你在商店看见朋友，想要知道他来商店做什么时，怎么问？
   Nǐ zài shāngdiàn kànjian péngyou, xiǎng yào zhīdào tā lái shāngdiàn zuò shénme shí, zěnme wèn?

   When you meet a friend of yours in a store, what do you usually say to him if you want to know his purpose?

2. 出入境时，要向海关人员出示哪些证件？应该怎么说？
   Chū-rù jìng shí, yào xiàng hǎiguān rényuán chūshì nǎxiē zhèngjiàn? Yīnggāi zěnme shuō?

   What certificates should be shown to customs officials to go through exit-entry formalities? What do you say to them?

Lesson 02

取行李
Qǔ Xíngli
Claiming Luggage

你知道吗？
Do you know?

Like airports in other countries, the airports in China also have free luggage carts, which are under the charge of assigned workers. After landing, you can view the display screen and find out which conveyor belt to claim your luggage, or you can consult the airport staff if you are not sure. Take care of your own luggage and do not put any valuable stuff into a luggage cart, because the airline would only compensate you for the loss of some items as appropriate, but not the valuables like money and jewelry.

Claiming Luggage

生词 Vocabulary

❶ 航班	hángbān	n.	airline flight; scheduled flight
❷ 取	qǔ	v.	take; get; fetch
❸ 行李	xíngli	n.	luggage; baggage
❹ 行李带	xínglidài	np.	conveyor belt
❺ 行李车	xínglichē	np.	luggage cart

句型 Sentence Patterns

❶ ……在哪儿取行李？
  ……zài nǎr qǔ xíngli?

❷ 这儿有……吗？
  Zhèr yǒu……ma?

情景会话 Situational Conversations

I

[A passenger in this example wants to know where he can claim his luggage.]

旅客：请问，CA978航班在哪儿取行李？
Qǐngwèn, CA jiǔ qī bā hángbān zài nǎr qǔ xíngli?
Excuse me, where can I claim luggage from flight CA978?

9

工作人员甲：在第11号行李带上，在那边。
Zài dì-shíyī hào xínglidài shang, zài nàbian.
At Conveyor Belt No. 11, over there.

II

[A passenger needs a luggage cart.]

旅客：请问，这儿有行李车吗？
Qǐngwèn, zhèr yǒu xínglichē ma?
Excuse me, are there any luggage carts around here?

工作人员乙：有，在那儿。
Yǒu, zài nàr.
Yes, they are over there.

旅客：谢谢。
Xièxie.
Thank you.

工作人员乙：不客气。
Bú kèqi.
You're welcome.

 **常用表达法**
Useful Phrases and Expressions

1. CA978航班在哪儿取行李？
CA jiǔ qī bā hángbān zài nǎr qǔ xíngli?
Where can I claim luggage from flight CA978?

After getting off the plane, you will certainly want to get your luggage. But where? You can ask a question like: "…… zài nǎr qǔ xíngli?" The following are more examples:

Claiming Luggage

❶ CZ167航班在哪儿取行李？
   CZ yāo liù qī hángbān zài nǎr qǔ xíngli?
   Where can I claim luggage from flight CZ167?

❷ MF623航班在哪儿取行李？
   MF liù èr sān hángbān zài nǎr qǔ xíngli?
   Where can I claim luggage from flight MF623?

2. 这儿有行李车吗？
   Zhèr yǒu xínglichē ma?
   Are there any luggage carts around here?

When you need a luggage cart or some other things, you can ask a question like: "Zhèr yǒu……ma?" Here are more examples:

❶ 这儿有行李寄存处吗？
   Zhèr yǒu xíngli jìcúnchù ma?
   Is there a left-luggage office around here?

❷ 这儿有出租车吗？
   Zhèr yǒu chūzūchē ma?
   Can I get a taxi around here?

练习
Exercises

一、读一读 Read the following words and phrases.

行李	xíngli	luggage
行李车	xínglichē	luggage cart
行李带	xínglidài	conveyor belt
行李寄存处	xíngli jìcúnchù	left-luggage office

出租车	chūzūchē	taxi
公共汽车	gōnggòng qìchē	bus
公用电话	gōngyòng diànhuà	public phone
轮船	lúnchuán	ship; boat
交通图	jiāotōngtú	traffic map

二、试一试 Substitution drills.

1. <u>CA978</u>航班在哪儿取行李?
   <u>CA jiǔ qī bā hángbān</u> zài nǎr qǔ xíngli?

   > HX336航班
   > HX sān sān liù hángbān
   >
   > CZ158航班
   > CZ yāo wǔ bā hángbān
   >
   > KL892航班
   > KL bā jiǔ èr hángbān
   >
   > MU219航班
   > MU èr yāo jiǔ hángbān

2. 这儿有<u>行李车</u>吗?
   Zhèr yǒu <u>xínglichē</u> ma?

   > 行李寄存处
   > xíngli jìcúnchù
   >
   > 公共汽车
   > gōnggòng qìchē
   >
   > 出租车
   > chūzūchē
   >
   > 公用电话
   > gōngyòng diànhuà

三、能力训练 Practice your Chinese.

1. 你想问你坐的航班应该在哪儿取行李。

   Nǐ xiǎng wèn nǐ zuò de hángbān yīnggāi zài nǎr qǔ xíngli.

   You would like to know where to claim your luggage from the flight you took.

2. 你找不到行李车时,怎么问飞机场的工作人员?

   Nǐ zhǎo bu dào xínglichē shí, zěnme wèn fēijīchǎng de gōngzuò rényuán?

   You can't find a cart for your luggage. What would you say to the staff member at the airport to get one?

找 洗 手 间
Zhǎo Xǐshǒujiān
Looking for a Washroom

你知道吗?
Do you know?

In Chinese, there are many names for toilet, such as "洗手间"(washroom), "卫生间"(sanitary room) and "一号"(literally NO. 1), etc. In some formal occasions, people say "我去方便一下"(similar to "I have to answer the call of nature") or "我出去一下"(I need to go out for a minute), instead of "去厕所"(going to the toilet). Many toilets in public places are free, but still in some places they are not. And most public toilets don't provide toilet paper.

Looking for a Washroom

生词
Vocabulary

❶	洗手间	xǐshǒujiān	n.	toilet; restroom
❷	楼梯	lóutī	n.	stairs; stairway
❸	麻烦	máfan	n./v.	trouble/bother
❹	附近	fùjìn	n.	nearby
❺	厕所	cèsuǒ	n.	toilet

句型
Sentence Patterns

❶ 我要去一趟/一下……
   Wǒ yào qù yí tàng/yíxià……

❷ 附近有……吗?
   Fùjìn yǒu……ma?

情景会话
Situational Conversations

I

[In a restaurant, a man wants to go to the restroom.]

男士A: 对不起，我要去一趟洗手间。
Duìbuqǐ, wǒ yào qù yí tàng xǐshǒujiān.
Excuse me, I need to go to the restroom.

15

[To the waitress]

男士A：小姐，洗手间在哪儿？

Xiǎojiě, xǐshǒujiān zài nǎr?

Excuse me, where is the restroom?

服务员：洗手间在楼梯那边。

Xǐshǒujiān zài lóutī nàbian.

It's near the stairway.

男士A：谢谢。

Xièxie.

Thank you.

II

[On the street]

男士B：麻烦您，附近有厕所吗？

Máfan nín, fùjìn yǒu cèsuǒ ma?

Excuse me, is there a toilet nearby?

路 人：往前走。

Wǎng qián zǒu.

Go straight ahead.

男士B：谢谢。

Xièxie.

Thank you.

常用表达法

Useful Phrases and Expressions

1. 我要去一趟洗手间。

Wǒ yào qù yí tàng xǐshǒujiān.

I need to go to the restroom.

Looking for a Washroom

When you are with friends, and you want to go to the restroom, you can say: "Wǒ yào qù yí tàng xǐshǒujiān." You can also say: "Wǒ yào qù yíxià……" "yíxià" means it won't take a long time. The following are more examples:

❶ 我要去一趟/一下休息室。
   Wǒ yào qù yí tàng/yíxià xiūxishì.
   I need to go to the lounge for a while.

❷ 我要去一趟/一下办公室。
   Wǒ yào qù yí tàng/yíxià bàngōngshì.
   I need to go to the office for a moment.

2. 附近有厕所吗？
   Fùjìn yǒu cèsuǒ ma?
   Is there a toilet nearby?

There are different ways of saying toilet in Chinese. The ones in public places are called "cèsuǒ" or "wèishēngjiān"; those in hotels or restaurants are called "xǐshǒujiān". When you are in a public place and need to go to a restroom or some other specific place, you can ask: "Fùjìn yǒu……ma?" Here are more examples:

❶ 附近有饭馆吗？
   Fùjìn yǒu fànguǎn ma?
   Is there a restaurant nearby?

❷ 附近有电话吗？
   Fùjìn yǒu diànhuà ma?
   Is there a telephone booth nearby?

一、读一读 Read the following words and phrases.

洗手间	xǐshǒujiān	toilet; washroom
卫生间	wèishēngjiān	toilet; restroom
办公室	bàngōngshì	office
休息室	xiūxishì	common room of a faculty; lounge
吸烟室	xīyānshì	smoking room
公司	gōngsī	company
餐厅	cāntīng	cafeteria
饭馆	fànguǎn	restaurant
茶馆	cháguǎn	tea house
咖啡厅	kāfēitīng	coffee shop
酒吧	jiǔbā	bar

二、试一试 Substitution drills.

1. 我要去一下/一趟<u>洗手间</u>。
   Wǒ yào qù yíxià/yí tàng <u>xǐshǒujiān</u>.

> 休息室
> xiūxishì
>
> 办公室
> bàngōngshì
>
> 公司
> gōngsī
>
> 朋友那儿
> péngyou nàr

2. 附近有饭馆吗?
   Fùjìn yǒu fànguǎn ma?

   茶馆
   cháguǎn

   酒吧
   jiǔbā

   咖啡厅
   kāfēitīng

   卫生间
   wèishēngjiān

三、能力训练 Practice your Chinese.

1. 与朋友交谈时,你想去一趟厕所。你应该怎么说?
   Yǔ péngyou jiāotán shí, nǐ xiǎng qù yí tàng cèsuǒ. Nǐ yīnggāi zěnme shuō?

   What would you say when you want to go to the restroom during a conversation?

2. 在街上,你想找公共厕所时,应该怎么问?
   Zài jiē shang, nǐ xiǎng zhǎo gōnggòng cèsuǒ shí, yīnggāi zěnme wèn?

   What would you say when you are looking for a public toilet in the street?

Lesson 04

坐出租车

Zuò Chūzūchē

Taking a Taxi

你知道吗?
Do you know?

　　Taxi fare in China is calculated by mileage. Now in Beijing, the starting fare is RMB 10.00 *yuan*, covering an initial distance of 3 kilometers. For each additional kilometer, the unit fare is RMB 2.00 *yuan*. After 11:00 pm, however, the price is a little bit higher, with an initial fee of RMB 11.00 *yuan* and a unit fare of RMB 3.00 *yuan* for each additional kilometer. Before getting out of a taxi, remember to ask the taxi driver for a receipt, with which you can look for things missing or lodge a complaint in case of loss or an accident. Beijingers tend to use "north", "south", "east" and "west" to give directions, so you'd better figure out the four directions rather than just knowing about the left and right.

Taking a Taxi

生词
Vocabulary

❶	表	biǎo	n.	meter
❷	发票	fāpiào	n.	bill; receipt
❸	高速公路	gāosù gōnglù	np.	expressway
❹	出口	chūkǒu	n.	exit
❺	拐	guǎi	v.	make a turn

句型
Sentence Patterns

❶ 去……多少钱?
Qù……duōshao qián?

❷ 走……,到出口往……拐。
Zǒu……, dào chūkǒu wǎng……guǎi.

情景会话
Situational Conversations

[A person wants to take a taxi to the airport.]

乘客:师傅,去机场多少钱?
Shīfu, qù jīchǎng duōshao qián?
Sir, how much is it to get to the airport?

司机：打表30多块钱。

Dǎ biǎo sānshí duō kuài qián.

Using the meter, it is around 30 *yuan*.

……

乘客：下车给我发票。

Xià chē gěi wǒ fāpiào.

Please give me a receipt when I get off.

II

[In the cab]

乘客：师傅，去国际俱乐部。

Shīfu, qù Guójì Jùlèbù.

Sir, please take me to the International Club.

司机：怎么走？

Zěnme zǒu?

Which way do you want to go?

乘客：走高速公路，到出口往右拐。

Zǒu gāosù gōnglù, dào chūkǒu wǎng yòu guǎi.

Take the expressway, and turn right at the exit.

常用表达法
Useful Phrases and Expressions

1. 去机场多少钱？

   Qù jīchǎng duōshao qián?

   How much is it to get to the airport?

You can use the structure "Qù……duōshao qián?" to ask how much you will have to pay to reach your destination. The following are more examples:

Taking a Taxi

❶ 去火车站多少钱?
Qù·huǒchēzhàn duōshao qián?
How much is it to get to the railway station?

❷ 去码头多少钱?
Qù mǎtou duōshao qián?
How much is it to get to the port?

2. 走高速公路，到出口往右拐。
Zǒu gāosù gōnglù, dào chūkǒu wǎng yòu guǎi.
Take the expressway, and turn right at the exit.

If you know how to get to your destination, you can give the driver directions using: "Zǒu……, dào……wǎng……guǎi." Here are more examples:

❶ 走高速公路，到出口往南拐。
Zǒu gāosù gōnglù, dào chūkǒu wǎng nán guǎi.
Take the expressway, and turn south at the exit.

❷ 走花园路，到路口往右拐。
Zǒu Huāyuán Lù, dào lùkǒu wǎng yòu guǎi.
Take the Huayuan Road, and turn right at the intersection.

练习
Exercises

一、读一读 Read the following words and phrases.

火车站	huǒchēzhàn	railway station
码头	mǎtou	port; dock
长途汽车站	chángtú qìchēzhàn	long-distance bus station

花园路	Huāyuán Lù	Huayuan Road
北京路	Běijīng Lù	Beijing Road
二环路	Èrhuán Lù	the Second Ring Road
长安街	Cháng'ān Jiē	Chang'an Avenue
立交桥	lìjiāoqiáo	flyover
左	zuǒ	left
右	yòu	right
东	dōng	east
南	nán	south
西	xī	west
北	běi	north
掉头	diào tóu	turn around

二、试一试 Substitution drills.

1. 去机场多少钱？
   Qù jīchǎng duōshao qián?

   长途汽车站
   chángtú qìchēzhàn

   码头
   mǎtou

   火车站
   huǒchēzhàn

   北京饭店
   Běijīng Fàndiàn

2. 走高速公路，到出口往右拐。
   Zǒu gāosù gōnglù, dào chūkǒu wǎng yòu guǎi.

花园路	往南拐
Huāyuán Lù	wǎng nán guǎi
北京路	往东拐
Běijīng Lù	wǎng dōng guǎi
四环路	往西拐
Sìhuán Lù	wǎng xī guǎi
长安街	往右拐
Cháng'ān Jiē	wǎng yòu guǎi
立交桥	掉头
lìjiāoqiáo	diào tóu

三、能力训练 Practice your Chinese.

1. 你想向出租汽车司机要发票，应该怎么说？
   Nǐ xiǎng xiàng chūzū qìchē sījī yào fāpiào, yīnggāi zěnme shuō?

   What would you say when you want to ask for a receipt from a taxi driver?

2. 你现在在哪里？从你现在的位置去市中心的西单商场怎么走？
   Nǐ xiànzài zài nǎli? Cóng nǐ xiànzài de wèizhì qù shì zhōngxīn de Xīdān Shāngchǎng zěnme zǒu?

   Where are you now? How can you get to Xidan Department Store from where you are?

Lesson 05

换 钱
Huàn Qián
Changing Money

Do you know?

In China, you are supposed to change your money in the designated banks or international hotels. Cash is normally exchanged at the latest rate of the current day, without any handling charge. No shops in any street run this business, nor do travel agencies. You can also cash traveler's checks in Bank of China, but need to pay some handling charges.

Changing Money

生词
Vocabulary

❶ 换	huàn	v.	exchange
❷ 数	shǔ	v.	count (money)
❸ 支票	zhīpiào	n.	check/cheque
❹ 面值	miànzhí	n.	denomination
❺ 钞票	chāopiào	n.	bill; bank note
❻ 签名	qiān míng	v.	sign one's name

句型
Sentence Patterns

❶ 今天……换多少人民币?
Jīntiān……huàn duōshao rénmínbì?

❷ 请给我……(面值)的钞票。
Qǐng gěi wǒ……(miànzhí) de chāopiào.

情景会话
Situational Conversations

I

[Here is a foreign student who wants to exchange money at the bank.]

留学生:小姐,今天1美元换多少人民币?
Xiǎojiě, jīntiān yì měiyuán huàn duōshao rénmínbì?
Miss, what is the exchange rate for one US dollar today?

Lesson 5

营业员：今天1美元换8.27元人民币。你换多少？
Jīntiān yì měiyuán huàn bā diǎn èr qī yuán rénmínbì. Nǐ huàn duōshao?
Today's rate is RMB 8.27 for one US dollar. How much do you want to exchange?

留学生：我换200美元。
Wǒ huàn èrbǎi měiyuán.
I want to exchange US $200.

营业员：一共是1654块，请数一下。
Yígòng shì yìqiān liùbǎi wǔshísì kuài, qǐng shǔ yíxià.
The total is 1,654 *yuan*. Please count it.

[Here, a customer wants to cash a traveler's check.]

顾　客：小姐，我想把这张支票换成人民币。
Xiǎojiě, wǒ xiǎng bǎ zhè zhāng zhīpiào huànchéng rénmínbì.
Miss, I would like to cash this check for RMB.

营业员：请把你的护照给我看一下。
Qǐng bǎ nǐ de hùzhào gěi wǒ kàn yíxià.
Please show me your passport.

顾　客：给你。请给我二十元和五十元面值的钞票。
Gěi nǐ. Qǐng gěi wǒ èrshí yuán hé wǔshí yuán miànzhí de chāopiào.
Here it is. Could I have it in twenty and fifty-*yuan* bills, please?

营业员：请你在这张纸上签一下名。
Qǐng nǐ zài zhè zhāng zhǐ shang qiān yíxià míng.
Please sign your name on this paper.

Changing Money

常用表达法
Useful Phrases and Expressions

1. 今天1美元换多少人民币?
   Jīntiān yì měiyuán huàn duōshao rénmínbì?
   What is the exchange rate for one US dollar today?

   When you are exchanging money at a bank or a hotel, you can ask for the exchange rate of foreign currencies by saying: "Jīntiān……huàn duōshao rénmínbì?" The following are more examples:

   ❶ 今天1英镑换多少人民币?
   Jīntiān yì yīngbàng huàn duōshao rénmínbì?
   What is the exchange rate for English pound today?

   ❷ 今天100日元换多少人民币?
   Jīntiān yìbǎi rìyuán huàn duōshao rénmínbì?
   What is the exchange rate for 100 Japanese yen today?

2. 请给我二十元和五十元面值的钞票。
   Qǐng gěi wǒ èrshí yuán hé wǔshí yuán miànzhí de chāopiào.
   Could I have it in twenty and fifty-yuan bills, please?

   If you want to exchange a sum of money for bills of a different denomination, you can say: "Qǐng gěi wǒ……(miànzhí)de chāopiào." Here are more examples:

   ❶ 请给我十元和二十元(面值)的钞票。
   Qǐng gěi wǒ shí yuán hé èrshí yuán (miànzhí) de chāopiào.
   Could I have it in ten and twenty-*yuan* bills, please?

   ❷ 请给我五块和十块的零钱。
   Qǐng gěi wǒ wǔ kuài hé shí kuài de língqián.
   Could I have the change in five and ten-*yuan* bills, please?

Exercises

一、读一读 Read the following words and phrases.

人民币	rénmínbì	RMB; Chinese currency
美元	měiyuán	US dollar
英镑	yīngbàng	British pound
日元	rìyuán	Japanese yen
欧元	ōuyuán	Euro
支票	zhīpiào	cheque; check
现金	xiànjīn	cash
零钱	língqián	small change; small value banknote
硬币	yìngbì	coin
信用卡	xìnyòngkǎ	credit card

二、试一试 Substitution drills.

1. 今天1美元换多少人民币？
   Jīntiān yì měiyuán huàn duōshao rénmínbì?

   1英镑
   yì yīngbàng

   1欧元
   yì ōuyuán

   100日元
   yìbǎi rìyuán

   500美元
   wǔbǎi měiyuán

Changing Money

2. 请给我二十元和五十元（面值）的钞票。
   Qǐng gěi wǒ èrshí yuán hé wǔshí yuán (miànzhí) de chāopiào.

一百元 yìbǎi yuán	现金 xiànjīn
两块和五块 liǎng kuài hé wǔ kuài	钞票 chāopiào
五千元 wǔqiān yuán	支票 zhīpiào
一元 yì yuán	硬币 yìngbì

三、能力训练 Practice your Chinese.

1. 去银行询问一下今天各种外币与人民币的兑换牌价是多少，并作记录。

   Qù yínháng xúnwèn yíxià jīntiān gèzhǒng wàibì yǔ rénmínbì de duìhuàn páijià shì duōshao, bìng zuò jìlù.

   Go to the bank to enquire exchange rates between foreign currencies and RMB and write them down.

2. 你要把旅行支票换成人民币现金，应该怎么说？

   Nǐ yào bǎ lǚxíng zhīpiào huànchéng rénmínbì xiànjīn, yīnggāi zěnme shuō?

   What would you say when you want to cash your traveller's check into RMB?

Lesson 06

天气
Tiānqì
Climate and Weather

你知道吗?
Do you know?

China stretches across a vast area, with the climate varying from place to place. In winter, the temperature gap between the northernmost and the southernmost regions may go up to 50℃. From television, newspapers, radio or Internet, you can learn about the weather of the following three days in all parts of the country; or you can call 12121, which provides weather forecast in both Chinese and English.

生词
Vocabulary

❶	天气	tiānqì	n.	weather
❷	预报	yùbào	v.	forecast
❸	晴	qíng	adj.	fine; clear
❹	转	zhuǎn	v.	turn; shift; change
❺	阴	yīn	adj.	overcast
❻	雨夹雪	yǔ jiā xuě	np.	rain and snow
❼	气温	qìwēn	n.	air temperature; atmospheric temperature
❽	度	dù	m.	degree
❾	多云	duōyún	n.	cloudy
❿	雾	wù	n.	fog

句型
Sentence Patterns

❶ 明天……，最高气温……度。
　Míngtiān……, zuì gāo qìwēn……dù.

❷ 明天有/没有……
　Míngtiān yǒu / méiyǒu……

33

情景会话
Situational Conversations

[Here are some people talking about the weather.]

女士：这几天天气真冷！

Zhè jǐ tiān tiānqì zhēn lěng!

The weather has been really cold lately!

男士：电视上的天气预报说，明天晴转阴，有雨夹雪，最高气温1度。

Diànshì shang de tiānqì yùbào shuō, míngtiān qíng zhuǎn yīn, yǒu yǔ jiā xuě, zuì gāo qìwēn yī dù.

I heard from the weather report on TV that tomorrow is going to be sunny to overcast with rain and snow. The highest temperature will be one degree.

女士：明天我去上海，不知道天气怎么样？

Míngtiān wǒ qù Shànghǎi, bù zhīdào tiānqì zěnmeyàng?

I am going to Shanghai tomorrow. I don't know what the weather is like there.

男士：上海明天阴转多云，有雾，但是气温比北京高，15度。

Shànghǎi míngtiān yīn zhuǎn duōyún, yǒu wù, dànshì qìwēn bǐ Běijīng gāo, shíwǔ dù.

Shanghai will be overcast to cloudy with fog tomorrow, but the temperature will be higher than that in Beijing. It will be fifteen degree.

女士：太好了，我不怕热，就怕冷。

Tài hǎo le, wǒ bú pà rè, jiù pà lěng.

That's great. I hate cold weather, but I don't mind the heat.

Climate and Weather

常用表达法
Useful Phrases and Expressions

1. 明天晴转阴，有雨夹雪，最高气温1度。
   Míngtiān qíng zhuǎn yīn, yǒu yǔ jiā xuě, zuì gāo qìwēn yī dù.
   Tomorrow is going to be sunny to overcast with rain and snow. The highest temperature will be one degree.

   Weather is one of the most common topics in many countries, and it is the same case in China. When listening to a weather report, we will usually hear something like: "Míngtiān qíng zhuǎn yīn, yǒu yǔ jiā xuě, zuì gāo qìwēn yī dù." Here are more useful examples:

   ❶ 明天阴，有雪，最高气温0度。
   Míngtiān yīn, yǒu xuě, zuì gāo qìwēn líng dù.
   Tomorrow is overcast with snow. The highest temperature is zero degree.

   ❷ 今天阴转晴，没有风，最高气温10度。
   Jīntiān yīn zhuǎn qíng, méiyǒu fēng, zuì gāo qìwēn shí dù.
   Today is overcast to sunny, and there is no wind. The highest temperature will be ten degree.

2. 上海明天阴转多云，有雾。
   Shànghǎi míngtiān yīn zhuǎn duōyún, yǒu wù.
   Shanghai will be overcast to cloudy with fog tomorrow.

   When listening to the weather forecast of a city, probably we will hear something like: "Shànghǎi míngtiān yīn zhuǎn duōyún, yǒu wù." Here are more examples:

   ❶ 北京明天阴，有雨。
   Běijīng míngtiān yīn, yǒu yǔ.
   Tomorrow it will be overcast and rainy in Beijing.

❷ 天津这几天多云,有雪。
Tiānjīn zhè jǐ tiān duōyún, yǒu xuě.
Over the next few days it will be cloudy and snowy in Tianjin.

练习
Exercises

一、读一读 Read the following words and phrases.

晴	qíng	fine; clear
阴	yīn	overcast
雨	yǔ	rain; rainy
雪	xuě	snow
雾	wù	fog
风	fēng	wind
沙尘	shāchén	small sand
多云	duōyún	cloudy
晴转阴	qíng zhuǎn yīn	sunny to overcast
雨夹雪	yǔ jiā xuě	rain and snow
(雷)阵雨	(léi)zhènyǔ	(thunder) shower
中到大雨	zhōng dào dà yǔ	moderate to heavy rain
阴转多云	yīn zhuǎn duōyún	overcast to cloudy
降水概率	jiàngshuǐ gàilǜ	probability of precipitation
最高气温	zuì gāo qìwēn	the highest temperature
最低气温	zuì dī qìwēn	the lowest temperature
1(摄氏)度	yī (Shèshì) dù	1 degree (Celsius)
15(摄氏)度	shíwǔ (Shèshì) dù	15 degree (Celsius)
30(摄氏)度	sānshí (Shèshì) dù	30 degree (Celsius)
华氏度	Huáshìdù	Fahrenheit

Climate and Weather

二、试一试 Substitution drills.

1. 明天 上海天气怎么样?
   Míngtiān Shànghǎi tiānqì zěnmeyàng?

今天 Jīntiān	东京 Dōngjīng
昨天 Zuótiān	北京 Běijīng
今天 Jīntiān	你们那里 nǐmen nàli
后天 Hòutiān	法国南部 Fǎguó nánbù

2. 明天 晴转阴, 有雨夹雪, 最高气温1度。
   Míngtiān qíng zhuǎn yīn, yǒu yǔ jiā xuě, zuì gāo qìwēn yī dù.

明天 Míngtiān	阴 yīn	有雾 yǒu wù	20 èrshí
今天 Jīntiān	多云 duōyún	没有风 méiyǒu fēng	12 shí'èr
后天 Hòutiān		有中到大雨 yǒu zhōng dào dà yǔ	15 shíwǔ
今天下午 Jīntiān xiàwǔ	晴 qíng	有阵雨 yǒu zhènyǔ	31 sānshíyī

3. 上海 明天 阴转多云, 有雾。
   Shànghǎi míngtiān yīn zhuǎn duōyún, yǒu wù.

天津 Tiānjīn	明天 míngtiān	多云转阴 duōyún zhuǎn yīn	小雪 xiǎo xuě
香港 Xiānggǎng	这几天 zhè jǐ tiān	多云 duōyún	雨 yǔ

| 广州 Guǎngzhōu | 今天 jīntiān | 晴 qíng | 风 fēng |
| 昆明 Kūnmíng | 明天 míngtiān | 晴转阴 qíng zhuǎn yīn | 大雨 dà yǔ |

三、能力训练 Practice your Chinese.

1. 你喜欢什么天气？不喜欢什么天气？
   Nǐ xǐhuan shénme tiānqì? Bù xǐhuan shénme tiānqì?
   What weather do you like? And what weather do you dislike?

2. 说说你所在的城市这几天的天气。
   Shuōshuo nǐ suǒ zài de chéngshì zhè jǐ tiān de tiānqì.
   Talk about what the weather has been like recently in your city.

预订房间

Yùdìng Fángjiān
Reserving a Room

Lesson 07

你知道吗?
Do you know?

With the development of China's tourist industry, the hotel industry in large and medium-sized cities also sees a boom. You can reserve a room through local travel agencies or on the Internet, or ask your friend in China to help you find a room in an affordable and good hotel. As specified by the Chinese government, only international hotels or hotels with international services are licensed to receive foreigners. In some cities like Beijing, though, there are some inexpensive youth hotels where foreign visitors can stay.

生词
Vocabulary

❶	预订	yùdìng	v.	reserve; make a reservation
❷	标准间	biāozhǔnjiān	np.	standard room
❸	空	kōng	adj.	vacant
❹	单人间	dānrénjiān	np.	single room
❺	套间	tàojiān	n.	suite

句型
Sentence Patterns

❶ 我想预订……
Wǒ xiǎng yùdìng……

❷ ……住一天多少钱？
……zhù yì tiān duōshao qián?

情景会话
Situational Conversations

I

[Here is a customer calling a hotel to reserve a room.]

服务员：您好！这里是长城饭店。
　　　　Nín hǎo! Zhèli shì Chángchéng Fàndiàn.
　　　　Hello! This is the Great Wall Hotel.

Reserving a Room

男　士：你好！我想预订一个标准间。
Nǐ hǎo! Wǒ xiǎng yùdìng yí ge biāozhǔnjiān.
Hello! I'd like to reserve a standard room.

服务员：您打算住多长时间？
Nín dǎsuan zhù duō cháng shíjiān?
How long do you plan to stay?

男　士：2月3号到7号。一天多少钱？
Èr yuè sān hào dào qī hào. Yì tiān duōshao qián?
From February the 3rd to the 7th. How much does it cost per night?

服务员：有50美元的，也有80美元的。
Yǒu wǔshí měiyuán de, yě yǒu bāshí měiyuán de.
We have 50 and 80-dollar standard rooms.

男　士：我要一间50美元的。
Wǒ yào yì jiān wǔshí měiyuán de.
I'll take a 50-dollar room.

II

[Here are a couple asking whether there is still a vacant room.]

男　士：你好，我们没有预订，请问这里有空房间吗？
Nǐ hǎo, wǒmen méiyǒu yùdìng, qǐngwèn zhèli yǒu kōng fángjiān ma?
Hello! We don't have a reservation. Are there any vacancies?

服务员：有，我们这儿有单人间、标准间和四人套间。
Yǒu, wǒmen zhèr yǒu dānrénjiān、biāozhǔnjiān hé sì rén tàojiān.
Yes. We have single rooms, standard rooms and four-person suites.

男 士：标准间住一天多少钱？

Biāozhǔnjiān zhù yì tiān duōshao qián?

How much does a standard room cost for one night?

服务员：268块。

Èrbǎi liùshíbā kuài.

Two hundred and sixty-eight *yuan*.

男 士：好，我们要一个标准间。

Hǎo, wǒmen yào yí ge biāozhǔnjiān.

OK. We'll take a standard room.

常用表达法
Useful Phrases and Expressions

1. 我想预订一个标准间。

   Wǒ xiǎng yùdìng yí ge biāozhǔnjiān.

   I would like to reserve a standard room.

When you want to reserve a room or make a reservation at a hotel, a restaurant or a travel agency over the phone or in person, you can say: "Wǒ xiǎng yùdìng……" The following are more examples:

❶ 我想预订两个单人间。

Wǒ xiǎng yùdìng liǎng ge dānrénjiān.

I would like to reserve two single rooms.

❷ 我想预订一个套间。

Wǒ xiǎng yùdìng yí ge tàojiān.

I would like to make a reservation for one suite.

2. 标准间住一天多少钱？

   Biāozhǔnjiān zhù yì tiān duōshao qián?

   How much does a standard room cost for one night?

Reserving a Room

When you want to reserve a hotel room, you can ask about a room's rate by saying: "……zhù yì tiān duōshao qián?" or "……zhù yí ge wǎnsè hang duōshao qián?" Here are some more examples:

❶ 单人间住一天多少钱?
Dānrénjiān zhù yì tiān duōshao qián?
What is the rate per night for a single room?

❷ 套间住一个晚上多少钱?
Tàojiān zhù yí ge wǎnshang duōshao qián?
What is the rate for a suite for one night?

练习
Exercises

一、读一读 Read the following words and phrases.

房间	fángjiān	room
标准间	biāozhǔnjiān	standard room
包间	bāojiān	small room at restaurant, theatre, etc.
火车票	huǒchēpiào	train ticket
飞机票	fēijīpiào	airplane ticket
套间	tàojiān	hotel suite
(三)星级	(sān) xīngjí	(three-)star
单人间	dānrénjiān	single room
双人间	shuāngrénjiān	double room
三人间	sānrénjiān	triple room
宿舍	sùshè	dormitory
公寓	gōngyù	apartment; flat

二、试一试 Substitution drills.

1. 我想预订<u>一个标准间</u>。
   Wǒ xiǎng yùdìng <u>yí ge biāozhǔnjiān</u>.

   一个包间
   yí ge bāojiān

   一个房间
   yí ge fángjiān

   一个三人间
   yí ge sānrénjiān

   一张飞机票
   yì zhāng fēijīpiào

2. <u>标准间</u>住一天/一个晚上多少钱？
   <u>Biāozhǔnjiān</u> zhù yì tiān / yí ge wǎnshang duōshao qián?

   套间
   Tàojiān

   宿舍
   Sùshè

   单人间
   Dānrénjiān

   这个房间
   Zhège fángjiān

三、能力训练 Practice your Chinese.

1. 你要预订一个每天20美元左右的房间，时间是下个月20日到25日。

   Nǐ yào yùdìng yí ge měi tiān èrshí měiyuán zuǒyòu de fángjiān, shíjiān shì xià ge yuè èrshí rì dào èrshíwǔ rì.

   You would like to reserve a $20-per-day room from the 20th to the 25th next month.

Reserving a Room

2. 请你询问一下当地三星级、四星级、五星级饭店标准间的价格，并进行比较。

Qǐng nǐ xúnwèn yíxià dāngdì sān xīngjí、sì xīngjí、wǔ xīngjí fàndiàn biāozhǔnjiān de jiàgé, bìng jìnxíng bǐjiào.

Enquire and compare the prices of a standard room in local three-star, four-star and five-star hotels.

Lesson 08

酒店登记
Jiǔdiàn Dēngjì
Checking in at a Hotel

你知道吗?
Do you know?

When checking in at a hotel in China, a foreigner should show his/her passport, fill in a registration form and pay a deposit. The registration form is written in both Chinese and English, so it doesn't matter if you do not read Chinese. The check-out time is usually before 12:00 am, but in some hotels, you can check out before 2:00 pm.

Checking in at a Hotel

生词
Vocabulary

❶	填	tián	v.	fill in
❷	住房登记卡	zhùfáng dēngjìkǎ	np.	registration form
❸	房卡	fángkǎ	n.	room card
❹	钥匙	yàoshi	n.	key
❺	押金	yājīn	n.	deposit
❻	结账	jié zhàng	v.	settle the bill
❼	退房	tuì fáng	vp.	check out of the hotel

句型
Sentence Patterns

❶ ……你看这样写对吗？
　　……nǐ kàn zhèyàng xiě duì ma?

❷ ……什么时候可以……？
　　……shénme shíhou kěyǐ……?

情景会话
Situational Conversations

I

[Here is a customer asking how to fill in the registration form.]

服务员：您需要填一张住房登记卡。在这里写上您的名字。

Nín xūyào tián yì zhāng zhùfáng dēngjìkǎ. Zài zhèli xiěshang nín de míngzi.

You need to fill in a registration form. Please write your name here.

47

旅　客：姓名、护照号码、居住时间，你看这样写对吗？

Xìngmíng、hùzhào hàomǎ、jūzhù shíjiān, nǐ kàn zhèyàng xiě duì ma?

Have I written my name, passport number and length of stay correctly?

服务员：对。这是您的房卡，请拿好。

Duì. Zhè shì nín de fángkǎ, qǐng náhǎo.

That's correct. Here is your room card. Please don't lose it.

II

[Here, a customer is asking some questions at the reception counter.]

服务员：请填写一下你的姓名和护照号码，还要交50块钱的钥匙押金。

Qǐng tiánxiě yíxià nǐ de xìngmíng hé hùzhào hàomǎ, háiyào jiāo wǔshí kuài qián de yàoshi yājīn.

Please write your name and passport number here. You also need to leave a 50-*yuan* deposit for the key.

旅　客：给你。我明天什么时候可以结账？退房的时候押金还给我吗？

Gěi nǐ. Wǒ míngtiān shénme shíhou kěyǐ jié zhàng? Tuì fáng de shíhou yājīn huángěi wǒ ma?

Here they are. What time can I check out tomorrow? Will you return the deposit to me when I check out?

服务员：中午12点以前结账，押金退房的时候还。

Zhōngwǔ shí'èr diǎn yǐqián jié zhàng, yājīn tuì fáng de shíhou huán.

You may check out before 12:00 pm. The deposit will be returned to you when you check out.

Checking in at a Hotel

常用表达法
Useful Phrases and Expressions

1. 姓名、护照号码，你看这样写对吗？
   Xìngmíng、hùzhào hàomǎ, nǐ kàn zhèyàng xiě duì ma?
   Have I written my name and passport number correctly?

   In China, a foreigner is supposed to write his/her name, identification number or passport number and length of stay in the registration form when checking into a hotel. If he/she wants to know whether he/she has correctly filled in the information in the registration form, he/she can ask a question like: "……nǐ kàn zhèyàng xiě duì ma?" The following are more examples:

   ❶ 姓名、电话，你看这样写对吗？
   Xìngmíng、diànhuà, nǐ kàn zhèyàng xiě duì ma?
   Have I written my name and telephone number correctly?

   ❷ 姓名、地址，你看这样写对吗？
   Xìngmíng、dìzhǐ, nǐ kàn zhèyàng xiě duì ma?
   Have I written my name and address correctly?

2. 我明天什么时候可以结账？
   Wǒ míngtiān shénme shíhou kěyǐ jié zhàng?
   What time can I check out tomorrow?

   When you want to ask when you can or should do something, you can ask a question like this: "……shénme shíhou kěyǐ……?" Here are more examples:

   ❶ 餐厅什么时候（可以）开门？
   Cāntīng shénme shíhou (kěyǐ) kāi mén?
   When is the dining room/restaurant open?

❷ 你们什么时候(可以)打扫房间?
Nǐmen shénme shíhou (kěyǐ) dǎsǎo fángjiān?
What time can you clean up the room?

练习
Exercises

一、读一读 Read the following words and phrases.

姓名	xìngmíng	name
地址	dìzhǐ	address
性别	xìngbié	gender
国籍	guójí	nationality
出生年月	chūshēng niányuè	date of birth
电话号码	diànhuà hàomǎ	telephone number
护照号码	hùzhào hàomǎ	passport number
房间号码	fángjiān hàomǎ	room number
居住时间	jūzhù shíjiān	length of stay

二、试一试 Substitution drills.

1. <u>姓名</u>、<u>护照号码</u>,你看这样写对吗?
   <u>Xìngmíng</u>、<u>hùzhào hàomǎ</u>, nǐ kàn zhèyàng xiě duì ma?

> 姓名、地址
> Xìngmíng、dìzhǐ
>
> 姓名、国籍、电话号码
> Xìngmíng、guójí、diànhuà hàomǎ
>
> 姓名、性别、国籍
> Xìngmíng、xìngbié、guójí
>
> 姓名、性别、出生年月
> Xìngmíng、xìngbié、chūshēng niányuè

Checking in at a Hotel

2. <u>我</u> <u>明天什么时候</u>（可以）<u>结账</u>？
   Wǒ míngtiān shénme shíhou (kěyǐ) jié zhàng?

你 Nǐ	来 lái
我 Wǒ	换钱 huàn qián
我们 Wǒmen	退房 tuì fáng
他 Tā	还钥匙 huán yàoshi

三、能力训练 Practice your Chinese.

1. 你想问朋友你写的地址对不对，应该怎么说？
   Nǐ xiǎng wèn péngyou nǐ xiě de dìzhǐ duì bu duì, yīnggāi zěnme shuō?

   If you want to ask your friend if the address you wrote is correct, what should you say?

2. 你问一下服务员，什么时候可以去餐厅吃饭？如果早上6点要去机场，什么时候可以结账？
   Nǐ wèn yíxià fúwùyuán, shénme shíhou kěyǐ qù cāntīng chī fàn? Rúguǒ zǎoshang liù diǎn yào qù jīchǎng, shénme shíhou kěyǐ jié zhàng?

   Ask the receptionist when you can go to the dining room for dinner, and what time you can check out if you go to the airport at 6:00 am.

Lesson 09

换房与报修

Huàn Fáng Yǔ Bàoxiū

Changing Rooms and Reporting a Repair

你知道吗?
Do you know?

If anything goes wrong with your room or the facilities in your room, no matter it is in an apartment, or a dorm, or a hotel room, you can report to the property management and ask for replacement or repair. But if you break anything in the room, you have to compensate for it at the original price.

Changing Rooms and Reporting a Repair

生词
Vocabulary

❶	租	zū	v.	rent
❷	修	xiū	v.	repair; fix
❸	下水道	xiàshuǐdào	n.	drain; sewer
❹	堵	dǔ	v.	block up (of toilets or kitchen)
❺	灯	dēng	n.	light
❻	派	pài	v.	send; dispatch

句型
Sentence Patterns

❶ 我房间的……坏了。
Wǒ fángjiān de……huài le.

❷ 请你找人帮我……
Qǐng nǐ zhǎo rén bāng wǒ……

情景会话
Situational Conversations

I

[Here, a foreign student asks a staff member for help.]

留学生: 小姐，我房间的窗户关不上。我可以换一个房间吗？
Xiǎojiě, wǒ fángjiān de chuānghu guān bu shàng. Wǒ kěyǐ huàn yí ge fángjiān ma?
Miss, the window in my room can't close. May I change to a different room?

53

服务员：您住几号房间？

Nín zhù jǐ hào fángjiān?

What is your room number?

留学生：127。

Yāo èr qī.

One Two Seven.

服务员：对不起，单人间都租出去了，有双人间，您要吗？

Duìbuqǐ, dānrénjiān dōu zū chūqu le, yǒu shuāngrénjiān, nín yào ma?

Sorry. The single rooms are all occupied. There are only double rooms. Do you want one?

留学生：那算了，你找人帮我修一下吧。

Nà suàn le, nǐ zhǎo rén bāng wǒ xiū yíxià ba.

In that case, please send somebody to fix it.

II

[Here is a customer calling the receptionist for help.]

旅　客：小姐，我房间里没有热水。

Xiǎojiě, wǒ fángjiān li méiyǒu rèshuǐ.

Miss, I do not have hot water in my room.

服务员：我们马上给您送。

Wǒmen mǎshàng gěi nín sòng.

We will send it to you right away.

旅　客：另外，房间厕所里的下水道堵住了，灯也不亮了，你能不能找人来修一下？

Lìngwài, fángjiān cèsuǒ li de xiàshuǐdào dǔzhù le, dēng yě bú liàng le, nǐ néng bu néng zhǎo rén lái xiū yíxià?

In addition, the drain in my bathroom is blocked and the light does not work. Can you send somebody to fix them?

服务员：我们马上派人去修。
Wǒmen mǎshàng pài rén qù xiū.
We will send someone to fix them immediately.

常用表达法
Useful Phrases and Expressions

1. 我房间的窗户关不上。
   Wǒ fángjiān de chuānghu guān bu shàng.
   The window in my room can't close.

   If anything in the room does not work properly, and you need it repaired or changed, you can let the hotel staff know by saying: "Wǒ fángjiān de……" The following are more examples:

   ❶ 我房间的门关不上。
   Wǒ fángjiān de mén guān bu shàng.
   The door in my room won't close.

   ❷ 我房间的电视机坏了。
   Wǒ fángjiān de diànshìjī huài le.
   The TV set in my room does not work.

2. 请你找人帮我修一下厕所的灯。
   Qǐng nǐ zhǎo rén bāng wǒ xiū yíxià cèsuǒ de dēng.
   Please get someone to come to repair the light in the bathroom.

   When you have a request or need someone to fix something in your room, you can ask the receptionist like: "Qǐng nǐ zhǎo rén bāng wǒ……" Here are more examples:

   ❶ 请你找人帮我修一下门。
   Qǐng nǐ zhǎo rén bāng wǒ xiū yíxià mén.
   Please send somebody to repair the door.

❷ 请你找人帮我换一个电视机。
  Qǐng nǐ zhǎo rén bāng wǒ huàn yí ge diànshìjī.
  Please send somebody to change the TV set.

练习
Exercises

一、读一读 Read the following words and phrases.

窗户	chuānghu	window
门	mén	door
锁	suǒ	lock
衣柜	yīguì	wardrobe
电视机	diànshìjī	television set
空调	kōngtiáo	air conditioner
冰箱	bīngxiāng	refrigerator
马桶	mǎtǒng	closestool; toilet
下水道	xiàshuǐdào	drain; sewer
水龙头	shuǐlóngtóu	water tap; faucet
浴缸	yùgāng	bathtub
灯	dēng	light
电话(机)	diànhuà (jī)	telephone (set)
检查	jiǎnchá	check

二、试一试 Substitution drills.

1. 我房间的<u>窗户关不上</u>。
   Wǒ fángjiān de <u>chuānghu guān bu shàng</u>.

   下水道堵了
   xiàshuǐdào dǔ le

Making a Telephone Call

灯坏了	dēng huài le
桌子坏了	zhuōzi huài le
电话坏了	diànhuà huài le

2. 请你找人帮我<u>修一下厕所的灯</u>。
   Qǐng nǐ zhǎo rén bāng wǒ <u>xiū yíxià cèsuǒ de dēng</u>.

修 xiū	下水道 xiàshuǐdào
修 xiū	空调 kōngtiáo
换 huàn	水龙头 shuǐlóngtóu
检查 jiǎnchá	电话 diànhuà

三、能力训练 Practice your Chinese.

1. 你房间的灯坏了，你怎么告诉服务员？
   Nǐ fángjiān de dēng huài le, nǐ zěnme gàosu fúwùyuán?

   How would you tell the receptionist that the light in your room does not work?

2. 房间里的冰箱坏了，请你通知饭店服务员或公寓管理员帮你换一台。
   Fángjiān li de bīngxiāng huài le, qǐng nǐ tōngzhī fàndiàn fúwùyuán huò gōngyù guǎnlǐyuán bāng nǐ huàn yì tái.

   The refrigerator in your room does not work. Ask an attendant of the hotel or the apartment manager to help you change it.

Lesson 10

打电话

Dǎ Diànhuà

Making a Telephone Call

你知道吗?
Do you know?

The scientific and technological development facilitates people's contact with each other. Telephones have made communication and exchange extremely convenient. Now telephones are highly popular in China. Almost every family has a telephone and everyone owns a cell phone. Some people even have two or three cell phones.

Making a Telephone Call

生词
Vocabulary

❶	空儿	kòngr	n.	free; free time
❷	聚会	jùhuì	n.	get-together; party
❸	参加	cānjiā	v.	take part in
❹	分机	fēnjī	n.	extension
❺	出去	chūqu	v.	go out

句型
Sentence Patterns

❶ ……你有空儿吗?
……nǐ yǒu kòngr ma?

❷ ……,你有什么事吗?
……, nǐ yǒu shénme shì ma?

情景会话
Situational Conversations

[Here, a man is calling his friend.]

王军: 喂,请问,是新东方学校吗?
Wèi, qǐngwèn, shì Xīndōngfāng Xuéxiào ma?
Hello. Is that New Oriental School?

女士：对，你找谁？
Duì, nǐ zhǎo shéi?
Yes. Whom do you want to speak to?

王军：请问，杰克先生在吗？
Qǐngwèn, Jiékè xiānsheng zài ma?
May I speak to Jack, please?

女士：请稍等。杰克，电话。
Qǐng shāo děng. Jiékè, diànhuà.
Wait a moment, please. Jack, your telephone.

……

杰克：喂，你好，我是杰克。你是哪位？
Wèi, nǐ hǎo, wǒ shì Jiékè. Nǐ shì nǎ wèi?
Hello, this is Jack. Who is that?

王军：我是王军。你们的电话太难打了，我打了好几次才打通。
Wǒ shì Wáng Jūn. Nǐmen de diànhuà tài nán dǎ le, wǒ dǎle hǎo jǐ cì cái dǎtōng.
This is Wang Jun. Your line is quite busy. I have tried calling you several times.

杰克：对不起。你有什么事吗？
Duìbuqǐ. Nǐ yǒu shénme shì ma?
Sorry. What's going on?

王军：周六晚上你有空儿吗？我和我的朋友有一个聚会，想请你来参加。
Zhōuliù wǎnshang nǐ yǒu kòngr ma? Wǒ hé wǒ de péngyou yǒu yí ge jùhuì, xiǎng qǐng nǐ lái cānjiā.
Are you free this Saturday evening? My friends and I would like to invite you to come to our party.

杰克：好，我一定去。

Hǎo, wǒ yídìng qù.

OK. I'll be there.

II

[Here, a woman is making a phone call.]

女士：喂，请接分机2694。

Wèi, qǐng jiē fēnjī èr liù jiǔ sì.

Hello. Extension 2694, please.

……

男士：喂？你找谁？

Wèi? Nǐ zhǎo shéi?

Hello? Who are you looking for?

女士：请问王军在吗？

Qǐngwèn Wáng Jūn zài ma?

Is Wang Jun in?

男士：他出去了，可能晚上才回来。你有什么事情要转告吗？

Tā chūqu le, kěnéng wǎnshang cái huílai. Nǐ yǒu shénme shìqing yào zhuǎngào ma?

He's out. He might be back in the evening. Do you want to leave a message for him?

女士：我是他妈妈，麻烦你让他回来后给家里打个电话。

Wǒ shì tā māma, máfan nǐ ràng tā huílai hòu gěi jiāli dǎ ge diànhuà.

I am his mother. Please ask him to call home when he comes back.

男士：没问题。

Méi wèntí.

No problem.

 **常用表达法**

Useful Phrases and Expressions

1. 周六晚上你有空儿吗?
   Zhōuliù wǎnshang nǐ yǒu kòngr ma?
   Are you free this Saturday evening?

   The question "……nǐ yǒu kòngr ma?" is used to make an invitation. The following are more examples:

   ❶ 明天下午你有空儿吗?
   Míngtiān xiàwǔ nǐ yǒu kòngr ma?
   Are you free tomorrow afternoon?

   ❷ 下个星期四你有空儿吗?
   Xià ge xīngqīsì nǐ yǒu kòngr ma?
   Are you free next Thursday?

2. 他不在,你有什么事情要转告吗?
   Tā bú zài, nǐ yǒu shénme shìqing yào zhuǎngào ma?
   He is not in. Do you want to leave a message for him?

   When you pick up an incoming call, but it is not for you, and the person it is for is not in, you may ask the caller if he/she wishes to leave a message. You can ask: "……nǐ yǒu shénme shìqing yào zhuǎngào ma?" Here are more examples:

   ❶ 他出去了,你有什么事情要转告吗?
   Tā chūqu le, nǐ yǒu shénme shìqing yào zhuǎngào ma?
   He's out. Do you want to leave a message for him?

   ❷ 他回家了,你有什么事情要转告吗?
   Tā huí jiā le, nǐ yǒu shénme shìqing yào zhuǎngào ma?
   He's already gone home. Do you want to leave a message for him?

Making a Telephone Call

练习
Exercises

一、读一读 Read the following words and phrases.

星期一（二、三……）	xīngqīyī (èr, sān…)	Monday (Tuesday, Wednesday…)
星期天/日	xīngqītiān/rì	Sunday
周一（二、三……）	zhōuyī (èr, sān…)	Monday (Tuesday, Wednesday…)
周日	zhōurì	Sunday
下周一	xià zhōuyī	next Monday
下个星期四	xià ge xīngqīsì	next Thursday
周末	zhōumò	weekend
早上	zǎoshang	early morning
上午	shàngwǔ	morning; forenoon
中午	zhōngwǔ	noon; midday
下午	xiàwǔ	afternoon
晚上	wǎnshang	evening; night
聚会	jùhuì	get-together; party
酒会	jiǔhuì	cocktail party
郊游	jiāoyóu	picnic; outing
出去	chūqu	go out
回家	huí jiā	go home
开会	kāi huì	have a meeting

二、试一试 Substitution drills.

1. 周六晚上你有空儿吗？
   Zhōuliù wǎnshang nǐ yǒu kòngr ma?

   星期五
   Xīngqīwǔ

下周四晚上
Xià zhōusì wǎnshang

明天早上8点
Míngtiān zǎoshang bā diǎn

这个周末
Zhège zhōumò

2. 他<u>不在</u>，你有什么事情要转告吗？
Tā bú zài, nǐ yǒu shénme shìqing yào zhuǎngào ma?

在开会
zài kāi huì

在上课
zài shàng kè

在洗澡
zài xǐ zǎo

去公司了
qù gōngsī le

三、能力训练 Practice your Chinese.

1. 打电话约朋友星期六晚上去电影院看电影。
Dǎ diànhuà yuē péngyou xīngqīliù wǎnshang qù diànyǐngyuàn kàn diànyǐng.
Call a friend and ask him/her to go to a movie on Saturday evening.

2. 你接了一个电话，这个人要找你的朋友，可是你的朋友不在，你怎么告诉那个人？怎么问他是否需要留言？
Nǐ jiēle yí ge diànhuà, zhège rén yào zhǎo nǐ de péngyou, kěshì nǐ de péngyou bú zài, nǐ zěnme gàosu nàge rén? Zěnme wèn tā shìfǒu xūyào liú yán?
You are receiving a phone call. The person on the phone says that he would like to speak to your friend, but your friend is not in. How would you tell the person? How would you ask him if he wants to leave a message?

留言

Liú Yán

Leaving a Message

Do you know?

Hotels in China are highly internationalized. At the front desk, you can leave a message to your visitors and get a message left for you. Besides, the clerks at the front desk are able to answer the common questions about the district and the city. So consult them whenever you have such questions.

生词
Vocabulary

1. 亲戚　　qīnqi　　n.　relatives
2. 转告　　zhuǎngào　v.　pass on a message (to a person)
3. 口信　　kǒuxìn　　n.　oral message

句型
Sentence Patterns

1. 请你转告……
   Qǐng nǐ zhuǎngào……

2. 我想给……留个口信。
   Wǒ xiǎng gěi……liú ge kǒuxìn.

情景会话
Situational Conversations

I

[Here is a customer leaving a message at the reception counter.]

客　人：小姐，下午我的亲戚要来看我，请你转告他我下午4点回来。

Xiǎojiě, xiàwǔ wǒ de qīnqi yào lái kàn wǒ, qǐng nǐ zhuǎngào tā wǒ xiàwǔ sì diǎn huílai.

Miss, a relative of mine will come to see me this afternoon. Please tell him that I will be back at 4:00 pm.

Leaving a Message

服务员：好的，没问题。
Hǎo de, méi wèntí.
Ok, no problem.

客　人：谢谢！
Xièxie!
Thanks!

服务员：再见。
Zàijiàn.
See you.

II

[Here, a man has come to see his friend, but his friend has gone out. So, he is leaving a message for his friend at the front desk.]

客　人：小姐，我想给415房间的客人留个口信。
Xiǎojiě, wǒ xiǎng gěi sì yāo wǔ fángjiān de kèrén liú ge kǒuxìn.
Miss, I would like to leave a message for the guest in Room 415.

服务员：好的。
Hǎo de.
All right.

客　人：我姓王，麻烦你告诉他，明天这个时候我再来看他。
Wǒ xìng Wáng, máfan nǐ gàosu tā, míngtiān zhège shíhou wǒ zài lái kàn tā.
My surname is Wang. Please tell him that I will come to see him again at this time tomorrow.

67

常用表达法
Useful Phrases and Expressions

1. 请你转告他我下午4点回来。
   Qǐng nǐ zhuǎngào tā wǒ xiàwǔ sì diǎn huílai.
   Please tell him that I will be back at 4:00 pm.

Someone is coming to see you at the hotel, but you have to go out. So, you will need to leave a message at the reception desk. You can ask the receptionist to convey your message to that person like: "Qǐng nǐ zhuǎngào……" The following are more examples:

❶ 请你转告他我回家了。
   Qǐng nǐ zhuǎngào tā wǒ huí jiā le.
   Please tell him I have already left for home.

❷ 请你转告他我明天再来看他。
   Qǐng nǐ zhuǎngào tā wǒ míngtiān zài lái kàn tā.
   Please tell him I will come to see him again tomorrow.

2. 我想给415房间的客人留个口信。
   Wǒ xiǎng gěi sì yāo wǔ fángjiān de kèrén liú ge kǒuxìn.
   I would like to leave a message for the guest in Room 415.

If you go to visit a friend, and he/she is not in, you will want to leave a message. You can say: "Wǒ xiǎng gěi……liú ge kǒuxìn." Here are more examples:

❶ 我想给415宿舍的张先生留个口信。
   Wǒ xiǎng gěi sì yāo wǔ sùshè de Zhāng xiānsheng liú ge kǒuxìn.
   I would like to leave a message for Mr. Zhang in Room 415.

❷ 我想给你们的张经理留个口信。
　　Wǒ xiǎng gěi nǐmen de Zhāng jīnglǐ liú ge kǒuxìn.
　　I would like to leave a message for your manager, Mr./Ms. Zhang.

练习
Exercises

一、读一读 Read the following words and phrases.

同屋	tóngwū	roommate
同事	tóngshì	colleague
回来	huílai	come back
回家	huí jiā	go home
回去	huíqu	go back
出来	chūlai	come out
出去	chūqu	go out
出差	chū chāi	go or be on a business trip
去商店	qù shāngdiàn	go to a shop/store
在家	zài jiā	at home
在学校	zài xuéxiào	at school
在公司	zài gōngsī	in the company
在饭店	zài fàndiàn	at the hotel

二、试一试 Substitution drills.

1. 请你转告他，我下午4点回来。
　　Qǐng nǐ zhuǎngào tā, wǒ xiàwǔ sì diǎn huílai.

张先生 Zhāng xiānsheng	出去了 chūqu le
小王 Xiǎo Wáng	去学校了 qù xuéxiào le

我朋友　　　　　下午在公司
wǒ péngyou　　 xiàwǔ zài gōngsī

王经理　　　　　明天去看他
Wáng jīnglǐ　　 míngtiān qù kàn tā

2. 我想给415房间的客人留个口信。
   Wǒ xiǎng gěi sì yāo wǔ fángjiān de kèrén liú ge kǒuxìn.

217宿舍的同学
èr yāo qī sùshè de tóngxué

公司的王经理
gōngsī de Wáng jīnglǐ

学校的李老师
xuéxiào de Lǐ lǎoshī

我的同屋
wǒ de tóngwū

三、能力训练 Practice your Chinese.

1. 你让阿里的同屋告诉阿里，你下午2点来找他。
   Nǐ ràng Ālǐ de tóngwū gàosu Ālǐ, nǐ xiàwǔ liǎng diǎn lái zhǎo tā.

   Ask Ali's roommate to tell Ali you are coming to meet him at 2:00 pm.

2. 请朋友的同事告诉你的朋友，你明天出差去上海。
   Qǐng péngyou de tóngshì gàosu nǐ de péngyou, nǐ míngtiān chū chāi qù Shànghǎi.

   Ask the colleague of your friend to tell him you are going on a business trip to Shanghai tomorrow.

Lesson 12

找人
Zhǎo Rén
Visiting Someone

你知道吗?
Do you know?

Chinese people used to visit each other whenever they like, but now they would make a phone call or an appointment first to make sure the person they are going to visit is not occupied at that time. Before meeting someone for business, you should also make an appointment through his/her secretary in advance; otherwise it would be impolite.

生词
Vocabulary

❶	前天	qiántiān	n.	the day before yesterday
❷	预约	yùyuē	v.	make an appointment
❸	办公室	bàngōngshì	n.	office

句型
Sentence Patterns

❶ 我想找一个人，……
Wǒ xiǎng zhǎo yí ge rén,……

❷ 我……预约（了）。
Wǒ……yùyuē (le).

情景会话
Situational Conversations

Ⅰ

[Here is a man coming to see Mike.]

客　人：小姐，我想找一个人，他叫Mike，美国人，是前天来的。

Xiǎojiě, wǒ xiǎng zhǎo yí ge rén, tā jiào Mike, Měiguórén, shì qiántiān lái de.

Miss, I want to see a man named Mike, an American. He arrived the day before yesterday.

服务员：他知道你要来吗？

Tā zhīdào nǐ yào lái ma?

Does he know you are coming?

客　人：知道。

Zhīdào.

Yes, he does.

服务员：请等一下。

Qǐng děng yíxià.

Wait a moment, please.

……

Mike先生请您在这儿等一下，他马上就下来。

Mike xiānsheng qǐng nín zài zhèr děng yíxià, tā mǎshàng jiù xiàlai.

Mike asks you to wait for him here. He will come down immediately.

II

[Here, a man has come to a company to see Manager Wang.]

客人：小姐，我是长城公司的。我想找一下王经理。

Xiǎojiě, wǒ shì Chángchéng Gōngsī de. Wǒ xiǎng zhǎo yíxià Wáng jīnglǐ.

Miss, I am from Changcheng Company. I would like to see Manager Wang.

秘书：您预约了吗？

Nín yùyuēle ma?

Have you made an appointment?

客人：没有，他不知道我要来。

Méiyǒu, tā bù zhīdào wǒ yào lái.

No, he doesn't know I'm coming.

秘书：请等一下。

Qǐng děng yíxià.

Wait a moment, please.

王经理请您去他的办公室，他在217号房间。

Wáng jīnglǐ qǐng nín qù tā de bàngōngshì, tā zài èr yāo qī hào fángjiān.

Manager Wang asks you to go to his office. He is in Room 217.

常用表达法
Useful Phrases and Expressions

1. 我想找一个人，他叫Mike，美国人，是前天来的。
   Wǒ xiǎng zhǎo yí ge rén, tā jiào Mike, Měiguórén, shì qiántiān lái de.
   I want to see a man named Mike, an American. He arrived the day before yesterday.

You will surely have many Chinese friends when you are in China. When you need to visit them at the place where they work or live, you can start with this sentence: "Wǒ xiǎng zhǎo……" The following are more examples:

❶ 我想找415房间的Amy，英国人，是昨天来的。
   Wǒ xiǎng zhǎo sì yāo wǔ fángjiān de Amy, Yīngguórén, shì zuótiān lái de.
   I would like to see Amy in Room 415, a British woman. She arrived yesterday.

❷ 我想找你们公司的王经理。
   Wǒ xiǎng zhǎo nǐmen gōngsī de Wáng jīnglǐ.
   I would like to see Manager Wang of your company.

Visiting Someone

2. 我打电话预约了。
   Wǒ dǎ diànhuà yùyuē le.
   I made an appointment over the telephone.

When you plan to visit someone in a company or an organization, you need to make an appointment first. When you speak to the receptionist, you can say to him/her: "Wǒ……yùyuē (le)." If not, you can say: "Wǒ méiyǒu yùyuē." Here are more examples:

❶ 我发传真预约了。
   Wǒ fā chuánzhēn yùyuē le.
   I've made an appointment via fax.

❷ 我没有预约。
   Wǒ méiyǒu yùyuē.
   I didn't make an appointment.

练习
Exercises

一、读一读 Read the following words and phrases.

美国	Měiguó	USA
俄罗斯	Éluósī	Russia
英国	Yīngguó	UK
法国	Fǎguó	France
德国	Déguó	Germany
日本	Rìběn	Japan
韩国	Hánguó	South Korea
前天	qiántiān	the day before yesterday

昨天	zuótiān	yesterday
今天	jīntiān	today
明天	míngtiān	tomorrow
后天	hòutiān	the day after tomorrow
打电话	dǎ diànhuà	call; make a phone call
发传真	fā chuánzhēn	send a fax
发电子邮件	fā diànzǐ yóujiàn	send an e-mail

二、试一试 Substitution drills.

1. 我想找一个人，他叫<u>Mike</u>，<u>美国人</u>，<u>前天</u>来的。
   Wǒ xiǎng zhǎo yí ge rén, tā jiào <u>Mike</u>, <u>Měiguórén</u>, <u>qiántiān</u> lái de.

Lida	法国人	昨天
Lida	Fǎguórén	zuótiān
山田	日本人	今天
Shāntián	Rìběnrén	jīntiān
Alex	俄罗斯人	前天早上
Alex	Éluósīrén	qiántiān zǎoshang
金昌永	韩国人	今天下午
Jīn Chāngyǒng	Hánguórén	jīntiān xiàwǔ

2. 我<u>打电话</u>预约了。
   Wǒ <u>dǎ diànhuà</u> yùyuē le.

| 昨天发传真 |
| zuótiān fā chuánzhēn |
| 上个星期写信 |
| shàng ge xīngqī xiě xìn |
| 发电子邮件 |
| fā diànzǐ yóujiàn |

三、能力训练　Practice your Chinese.

1. 你在一个饭店想找一个人——John Taylor，他是昨天从加拿大来的。

   Nǐ zài yí ge fàndiàn xiǎng zhǎo yí ge rén ——John Taylor, tā shì zuótiān cóng Jiānádà lái de.

   You want to see a man named John Taylor at a hotel, who came yesterday from Canada.

2. 你告诉服务员，你要找饭店经理。

   Nǐ gàosu fúwùyuán, nǐ yào zhǎo fàndiàn jīnglǐ.

   Tell the receptionist that you want to see the manager of the hotel.

Lesson 13

洗衣
xǐ yī
Doing Laundry

你知道吗?
Do you know?

Laundry service is available in most hotels, and you have to pay for them. There are also many laundry shops outside the hotels in the street. Different types of clothes have different service prices. Generally, you can choose either washing or dry-cleaning, with the latter a little bit more expensive than the former. In China, coin-operated laundry machines are hard to find in laundry shops. Some foreign students' dorms and apartments have them though.

Doing Laundry

生词
Vocabulary

❶ 西装	xīzhuāng	n.	Western suit
❷ 毛料	máoliào	n.	woolen
❸ 内衣	nèiyī	n.	underclothes
❹ 油迹	yóujì	n.	oil stain
❺ 加急	jiājí	adj.	urgent

句型
Sentence Patterns

❶ 洗……需要多长时间？
Xǐ……xūyào duō cháng shíjiān?

❷ 这里还有……，没洗干净。
Zhèlǐ hái yǒu……, méi xǐ gānjìng.

情景会话
Situational Conversations

I

[Here, a customer has come to a laundry shop.]

客 人：请问，洗一件衣服需要多长时间？

Qǐngwèn, xǐ yí jiàn yīfu xūyào duō cháng shíjiān?

Excuse me, how long does it take to have an item of clothing cleaned?

79

服务员：一天。

Yì tiān.

One day.

客　人：洗西装也是一天吗？

Xǐ xīzhuāng yě shì yì tiān ma?

Does it also take one day to have a suit cleaned?

服务员：不，洗一般的衣服需要一天，洗毛料的衣服需要两天。

Bù, xǐ yìbān de yīfu xūyào yì tiān, xǐ máoliào de yīfu xūyào liǎng tiān.

No. It takes one day to wash ordinary material clothes and two days to clean woolen clothes.

客　人：请问你们洗内衣吗？

Qǐngwèn nǐmen xǐ nèiyī ma?

Do you wash underclothes?

服务员：对不起，我们不洗内衣。

Duìbuqǐ, wǒmen bù xǐ nèiyī.

Sorry, we don't wash underclothes.

[In a hotel, a lady's laundry is done.]

服务员：小姐，您的衣服洗好了。

Xiǎojiě, nín de yīfu xǐhǎo le.

Miss, your clothes are ready.

客　人：谢谢，我看一下。你看，这里还有油迹，没洗干净。

Xièxie, wǒ kàn yíxià. Nǐ kàn, zhèli hái yǒu yóujì, méi xǐ gānjìng.

Thank you. Let me have a look. Look, there is still an oil stain here. It has not been completely cleaned.

Doing Laundry

服务员：对不起，我告诉洗衣房再洗一次。明天给您行吗？
Duìbuqǐ, wǒ gàosu xǐyīfáng zài xǐ yí cì. Míngtiān gěi nín xíng ma?
Sorry. I will tell the laundry to wash it again. Can we bring it to you tomorrow?

客　人：明天我要穿。能不能快一点儿？
Míngtiān wǒ yào chuān. Néng bu néng kuài yìdiǎnr?
I need to wear it tomorrow. Can I get it back earlier?

服务员：好，我们有加急服务。
Hǎo, wǒmen yǒu jiājí fúwù.
All right. We will arrange an urgent service for you.

常用表达法
Useful Phrases and Expressions

1. 洗一件衣服需要多长时间？
   Xǐ yí jiàn yīfu xūyào duō cháng shíjiān?
   How long does it take to have an item of clothing cleaned?

Sometimes you need to go to a laundry shop to have your laundry done. What should you say in a laundry shop? Here is a useful expression when you want to know how long the laundry will take: "Xǐ……xūyào duō cháng shíjiān?" The following are more examples:

❶ 洗一套西装需要多长时间？
   Xǐ yí tào xīzhuāng xūyào duō cháng shíjiān?
   How long does it take to have a suit cleaned?

❷ 洗一条裤子需要多长时间？
   Xǐ yì tiáo kùzi xūyào duō cháng shíjiān?
   How long does it take to have a pair of pants washed?

2. 这里还有油迹，没洗干净。
   Zhèli hái yǒu yóujì, méi xǐ gānjìng.
   There is still an oil stain here. It has not been completely cleaned.

If there are still some stains left on your clothes when they are supposed to have been cleaned, you can tell the person who operates the laundry: "Zhèli hái yǒu……, méi xǐ gānjìng." Here are more examples:

❶ 这里还有黑点儿，没洗干净。
   Zhèli hái yǒu hēi diǎnr, méi xǐ gānjìng.
   There is still a black stain here. It has not been completely cleaned.

❷ 这里还有血迹，没洗干净。
   Zhèli hái yǒu xuèjì, méi xǐ gānjìng.
   There is still a blood stain here. It has not been completely cleaned.

练习
Exercises

一、读一读 Read the following words and phrases.

西装	xīzhuāng	business suit; Western suit
领带	lǐngdài	necktie; tie
外套	wàitào	coat
羽绒服	yǔróngfú	down wear
衬衣	chènyī	shirt
裤子	kùzi	pants; trousers
牛仔裤	niúzǎikù	jeans
裙子	qúnzi	skirt; dress
床单	chuángdān	bedspread

Doing Laundry

窗帘	chuānglián	curtain
油迹	yóujì	oil stain
黑点儿	hēi diǎnr	black stain
红点儿	hóng diǎnr	red stain
墨迹	mòjì	ink stain
血迹	xuèjì	blood stain

二、试一试 Substitution drills.

1. 洗<u>一件衣服</u>需要多长时间?
   Xǐ yí jiàn yīfu xūyào duō cháng shíjiān?

   一件衬衣
   yí jiàn chènyī

   一件外套
   yí jiàn wàitào

   一条裙子
   yì tiáo qúnzi

   一条裤子
   yì tiáo kùzi

2. 这里还有<u>油迹</u>,没洗干净。
   Zhèli hái yǒu yóujì, méi xǐ gānjìng.

   血迹
   xuèjì

   墨迹
   mòjì

   红点儿
   hóng diǎnr

   黑点儿
   hēi diǎnr

三、能力训练 Practice your Chinese.

1. 你问洗衣店的人洗你的衣服需要几天?

   Nǐ wèn xǐyīdiàn de rén xǐ nǐ de yīfu xūyào jǐ tiān?

   Ask the attendant in the laundry shop how many days it will take them to wash your clothes.

2. 告诉店员你的衣服还有油迹,没洗干净。

   Gàosu diànyuán nǐ de yīfu hái yǒu yóujì, méi xǐ gānjìng.

   Tell the attendant in the laundry shop that they did not wash your clothes well and there are still oil stains on the clothes.

结 账

Jié Zhàng

Paying the Bill

你知道吗?
Do you know?

Paying a bill at a shopping mall, a restaurant or a hotel is called "结账" in Mandarin Chinese and "买单" or "埋单" in Cantonese. Sometimes when a cashier is busy, he/she may overcharge or undercharge a customer as a result of a billing error, leading to really unpleasant situations. To prevent this kind of situations, you'd better check the bill carefully and point out anything that is confusing or wrong before you actually pay the bill. Some upscale places charge a 10%–15% service fee, but the waiters and waitresses seldom accept tips.

生词 Vocabulary

❶	收银台	shōuyíntái	np.	cashier desk
❷	账单	zhàngdān	n.	bill
❸	算	suàn	v.	calculate
❹	电话费	diànhuàfèi	np.	telephone charge
❺	哦	ò	int.	Oh (*indicating understanding or realization*)

句型 Sentence Patterns

❶ 我想……，请……
Wǒ xiǎng……, qǐng……

❷ 这……是什么钱？
Zhè……shì shénme qián?

情景会话 Situational Conversations

I

[Here is a customer checking out.]

客　人：小姐，我要结账。
　　　　Xiǎojiě, wǒ yào jié zhàng.
　　　　Miss, I want to check out.

Paying the Bill

服务员A: 先生，您请到这边收银台。

Xiānsheng, nín qǐng dào zhèbian shōuyíntái.

Sir, please come to the cashier desk here.

……

客　人: 小姐，我下午4点要去机场，我想现在结账，请您开好账单。

Xiǎojiě, wǒ xiàwǔ sì diǎn yào qù jīchǎng, wǒ xiǎng xiànzài jié zhàng, qǐng nín kāihǎo zhàngdān.

Miss, I will go to the airport at 4:00 pm. I would like to check out now. Please have my bill ready.

服务员B: 好，我算一下，请您等一会儿。

Hǎo, wǒ suàn yíxià, qǐng nín děng yíhuìr.

Yes. Let me work out the bill for you. Please wait for a moment.

……

一共是720块。

Yígòng shì qībǎi èrshí kuài.

The total is 720 *yuan*.

[Here is a customer checking his bill.]

服务员: 这是你的账单，一共1650块。

Zhè shì nǐ de zhàngdān, yígòng yìqiān liùbǎi wǔshí kuài.

Here is your bill. The total is 1,650 *yuan*.

客　人: 这么多？这150块是什么钱？

Zhème duō? Zhè yìbǎi wǔshí kuài shì shénme qián?

That much? What is this 150-*yuan* charge for?

87

服务员：这是你的电话费。
Zhè shì nǐ de diànhuàfèi.
That is your telephone charge.

客　人：哦，我明白了。
Ò, wǒ míngbai le.
Oh, I see.

常用表达法
Useful Phrases and Expressions

1. 我想现在结账，请您开好账单。
   Wǒ xiǎng xiànzài jié zhàng, qǐng nín kāihǎo zhàngdān.
   I would like to check out now. Please have my bill ready.

When you are about to check out of a hotel, you can use this structure to tell the receptionist that you want to check out and ask for the bill: "Wǒ xiǎng……, qǐng nǐ(nín)……" The following are more examples:

❶ 我想现在去机场，请你帮我叫出租车。
   Wǒ xiǎng xiànzài qù jīchǎng, qǐng nǐ bāng wǒ jiào chūzūchē.
   I want to go to the airport now. Please call a taxi for me.

❷ 我想明天去广州，请你帮我预订机票。
   Wǒ xiǎng míngtiān qù Guǎngzhōu, qǐng nǐ bāng wǒ yùdìng jīpiào.
   I would like to go to Guangzhou tomorrow. Please book an airline ticket for me.

2. 这150块是什么钱？
   Zhè yìbǎi wǔshí kuài shì shénme qián?
   What is this 150-*yuan* charge for?

Paying the Bill

When you find a charge on your bill and do not know what it is for, you can ask: "Zhè……shì shénme qián?" Here are more examples:

❶ 这15%是什么钱?

  Zhè bǎifēnzhī shíwǔ shì shénme qián?
  What is this 15% charge for?

❷ 这10块钱是什么钱?

  Zhè shí kuài qián shì shénme qián?
  What is this 10-*yuan* charge for?

练习
Exercises

一、读一读 Read the following words and phrases.

房费	fángfèi	rent
水费	shuǐfèi	water bill
电费	diànfèi	electricity bill
学费	xuéfèi	tuition
生活费	shēnghuófèi	cost of living
电话费	diànhuàfèi	telephone bill
服务费	fúwùfèi	service charge
机场建设费	jīchǎng jiànshèfèi	airport construction fee
保险费	bǎoxiǎnfèi	insurance premium
燃油费	rányóufèi	fuel surcharge
小费	xiǎofèi	tip
现金	xiànjīn	cash
信用卡	xìnyòngkǎ	credit card
支票	zhīpiào	check

二、试一试 Substitution drills.

1. 我想<u>现在结账</u>,请你<u>开好账单</u>。
   Wǒ xiǎng <u>xiànzài jié zhàng</u>, qǐng nǐ <u>kāihǎo zhàngdān</u>.

打个电话	帮我接总机
dǎ ge diànhuà	bāng wǒ jiē zǒngjī
去北京饭店	帮我叫出租车
qù Běijīng Fàndiàn	bāng wǒ jiào chūzūchē
明天去广州	帮我买火车票
míngtiān qù Guǎngzhōu	bāng wǒ mǎi huǒchēpiào
后天去长城公司	帮我预约一下
hòutiān qù Chángchéng Gōngsī	bāng wǒ yùyuē yíxià

2. 这<u>150块</u>是什么钱?
   Zhè <u>yìbǎi wǔshí kuài</u> shì shénme qián?

   60块
   liùshí kuài

   20%
   bǎifēnzhī èrshí

   300美元
   sānbǎi měiyuán

   15%和25%
   bǎifēnzhī shíwǔ hé bǎifēnzhī èrshíwǔ

三、能力训练 Practice your Chinese.

1. 你要在两个小时以后离开饭店去飞机场,现在你要结账,你问服务员能不能用信用卡结账。
   Nǐ yào zài liǎng ge xiǎoshí yǐhòu líkāi fàndiàn qù fēijīchǎng, xiànzài nǐ yào jié zhàng, nǐ wèn fúwùyuán néng bu néng yòng xìnyòngkǎ jié zhàng.

Paying the Bill

You are leaving the hotel for the airport in two hours. Now you want to check out and ask the receptionist whether the credit card can be used to pay the bill.

2. 找一张购物或餐饮的账单,说说看里面每一项都是什么钱。
Zhǎo yì zhāng gòu wù huò cānyǐn de zhàngdān, shuōshuo kàn lǐmiàn měi yí xiàng dōu shì shénme qián.

Find a shopping bill or a meal bill, and tell what each charge is for.

Lesson 15

问 路
Wèn Lù
Asking for Directions

你知道吗?
Do you know?

During your stay in China, you may go out and have fun with your friends on weekends. If you get lost, ask passers-by for directions and in most cases they will be delighted to show you the way. If your Chinese is not good, you'd better seek help from students or young people who may be able to explain to you in English.

Asking for Directions

生词
Vocabulary

❶	站	zhàn	n.	station; stop
❷	劳驾	láo jià	v.	excuse me
❸	列车	lièchē	n.	train
❹	站台	zhàntái	n.	platform (in a railway station)
❺	检票	jiǎn piào	v.	punch a ticket
❻	十字路口	shízì lùkǒu	np.	intersection

句型
Sentence Pattern

❶ ……在……
　　……zài……

❷ 去……怎么走?
　　Qù……zěnme zǒu?

情景会话
Situational Conversation

[Here, a traveler wants to know where the taxi station is.]

旅　客: 请问, 出租汽车站在哪儿?
　　　　Qǐngwèn, chūzū qìchēzhàn zài nǎr?
　　　　Excuse me, where is the taxi station?

93

工作人员：出租汽车站在大门外左边。

Chūzū qìchēzhàn zài dàmén wài zuǒbian.

The taxi station is on the left side of the main gate.

II

[At the railway station]

旅　　客：劳驾，北京到上海的31次列车在哪儿上车？

Láo jià, Běijīng dào Shànghǎi de sānshíyī cì lièchē zài nǎr shàng chē?

Excuse me, where can I get on Train No. 31 from Beijing to Shanghai?

工作人员：第二站台。

Dì-èr zhàntái.

At Platform No. 2.

旅　　客：在哪儿检票？

Zài nǎr jiǎn piào?

Where can I check in (get the ticket punched)?

工作人员：上二楼，左拐，第七检票口。

Shàng èr lóu, zuǒ guǎi, dì-qī jiǎnpiàokǒu.

Go up to the second floor, and turn left, at Gate No. 7.

III

[Cycling in the way]

旅客：请问，去颐和园怎么走？

Qǐngwèn, qù Yíhé Yuán zěnme zǒu?

Excuse me, can you tell me how to get to the Summer Palace?

路人：往前走，在第一个十字路口向北拐，再往前骑200米，右拐就是。

Wǎng qián zǒu, zài dì-yī ge shízì lùkǒu xiàng běi guǎi, zài wǎng qián qí èrbǎi mǐ, yòu guǎi jiù shì.

Go straight ahead. Turn north at the first intersection. Keep going forward for another 200 meters. Then turn right, and you will find it there.

常用表达法
Useful Phrases and Expressions

1. 出租汽车站在大门外左边。
   Chūzū qìchēzhàn zài dàmén wài zuǒbian.
   The taxi station is on the left side of the main gate.

In China, if you ask someone for directions, you should say: "……zài nǎr?" And he/she will answer you: "……zài……" You might get different guidance from different people. A Beijing resident would tell you the way by saying "*to the east*", "*to the west*", "*to the south*" or "*to the north*". But if you ask a southerner for a direction, he/she may tell you by saying "*go forward*", "*go backward*", "*to the left*" or "*to the right*". The following are more examples:

❶ 15路汽车站在学校前边100米。
   Shíwǔ lù qìchēzhàn zài xuéxiào qiánbian yìbǎi mǐ.
   The bus stop for Bus No.15 is about 100 meters away from the school's entrance.

❷ 我们公司在马路右边。
   Wǒmen gōngsī zài mǎlù yòubian.
   Our company is on the right side of the road.

2. 去颐和园怎么走?
   Qù Yíhé Yuán zěnme zǒu?
   Can you tell me how to get to the Summer Palace?

It can be quite an extraordinary experience to bike or stroll around cities in China because, in this way, you can get a glimpse of the daily life of Chinese people. If you want to know how to get to a specific place, you may ask: "Qù……zěnme zǒu?" Here are more examples:

❶ 去国际饭店怎么走?

Qù Guójì Fàndiàn zěnme zǒu?

Can you tell me the way to the International Hotel?

❷ 去中国银行怎么走?

Qù Zhōngguó Yínháng zěnme zǒu?

Can you tell me how to get to the Bank of China?

练习
Exercises

一、读一读 Read the following words and phrases.

前边	qiánbian	front side
后边	hòubian	back side
左边	zuǒbian	left side
右边	yòubian	right side
旁边	pángbiān	beside
对面	duìmiàn	opposite
附近	fùjìn	nearby
东边	dōngbian	east side
西边	xībian	west side
南边	nánbian	south side
北边	běibian	north side
中间	zhōngjiān	center

Asking for Directions

二、试一试 Substitution drills.

1. <u>出租汽车站</u>在<u>大门外左边</u>。
   Chūzū qìchēzhàn zài dàmén wài zuǒbian.

公共汽车站 Gōnggòng qìchēzhàn	学校前边 xuéxiào qiánbian
火车站 Huǒchēzhàn	北京饭店旁边 Běijīng Fàndiàn pángbiān
长城公司 Chángchéng Gōngsī	马路对面 mǎlù duìmiàn
中国银行 Zhōngguó Yínháng	北京饭店和友谊商场中间 Běijīng Fàndiàn hé Yǒuyì Shāngchǎng zhōngjiān

2. 去<u>颐和园</u>怎么走?
   Qù Yíhé Yuán zěnme zǒu?

故宫 Gùgōng
飞机场 fēijīchǎng
你们学校 nǐmen xuéxiào
花园路五号 Huāyuán Lù wǔ hào

三、能力训练 Practice your Chinese.

1. 你想问乘务员K186次列车在哪儿检票。
   Nǐ xiǎng wèn chéngwùyuán K yāo bā liù cì lièchē zài nǎr jiǎn piào.
   You want to ask an attendant where to check in for Train K186.

2. 向路人询问从你所在的地方去北京大学应该怎么走。

Xiàng lùrén xúnwèn cóng nǐ suǒ zài de dìfang qù Běijīng Dàxué yīnggāi zěnme zǒu.

Ask a passer-by how to get to Peking University from where you are.

乘 车
Chéng Chē
Means of Transportation

💡 **你知道吗?**
Do you know?

In China, buses and subways are the major means of transportation. There are air-conditioned buses and non-airconditioned buses, charging different fares. In some big cities, buses are beginning to adopt the system of self-service ticketing, requiring passengers to get on a bus at the front door and get off at the back door. If there is a conductor on the bus, you can buy your ticket from him/her; if there isn't one, you have to prepare and tender the exact fare. Many office workers use a commutation ticket or an IC card to pay the bus fare, while seniors can enjoy a free ride with a senior citizen identification card.

Subway ticketing systems differ from city to city. For example, Shanghai Subway uses a distance-based fare system, while Beijing Subway adopts a unified fare regardless of distance. China is a country with a huge population, so buses and subways are always overcrowded. If you want to experience a fun ride, you are suggested to avoid the rush hours.

Lesson 16

生词
Vocabulary

❶	过	guò	v.	pass; cross
❷	换(车)	huàn (chē)	v.	transfer buses (trains)
❸	地铁	dìtiě	n.	subway
❹	动物园	dòngwùyuán	n.	zoo
❺	过街天桥	guòjiē tiānqiáo	np.	overhead pedestrian crossing

句型
Sentence Patterns

❶ 去……怎么坐车?
Qù……zěnme zuò chē?

❷ 买……票,到……
Mǎi……piào, dào……

情景会话
Situational Conversations

I

[Here are three students going to Qianmen.]

留学生: 请问,去前门怎么坐车?
Qǐngwèn, qù Qiánmén zěnme zuò chē?
Excuse me, which bus should we take to Qianmen?

路　人：过马路，在右边那个车站坐102、103或者121路。

Guò mǎlù, zài yòubian nàge chēzhàn zuò yāo líng èr、yāo líng sān huòzhě yāo èr yāo lù.

Just cross the road, and take Bus No. 102, No. 103 or No. 121 at the bus stop on the right.

留学生：要换车吗？

Yào huàn chē ma?

Do I have to change buses?

路　人：在阜成门换地铁。

Zài Fùchéngmén huàn dìtiě.

You need to transfer to the subway at Fuchengmen.

留学生：谢谢。

Xièxie.

Thank you.

[After getting on the bus]

留学生：师傅，买三张票，到阜成门。

Shīfu, mǎi sān zhāng piào, dào Fùchéngmén.

Sir, I want to buy three tickets to Fuchengmen.

售票员：三块。

Sān kuài.

Three *yuan*.

[Here is a couple going to the zoo.]

男士：小姐，我们要去动物园，在哪儿坐车？

Xiǎojiě, wǒmen yào qù dòngwùyuán, zài nǎr zuò chē?

Miss, we want to go to the zoo. Where should we take the bus?

路人：从这儿坐102，到阜成门换103。

Cóng zhèr zuò yāo líng èr, dào Fùchéngmén huàn yāo líng sān.

Take Bus No. 102 from here, and then transfer to Bus No. 103 at Fuchengmen.

男士：车站在哪儿？

Chēzhàn zài nǎr?

Where is the bus stop?

路人：下过街天桥就是。

Xià guòjiē tiānqiáo jiù shì.

Just under the overhead pedestrian crossing.

常用表达法
Useful Phrases and Expressions

1. 去前门怎么坐车？

   Qù Qiánmén zěnme zuò chē?

   Which bus should we take to Qianmen?

We have different types of public transportation. We have buses, double-deckers, air-conditioned buses, subway trains, etc. If you are new to a city, you can read guideboards or maps at the station. Or you may ask a pedestrian: "Qù……zěnme zuò chē?" The following are more examples:

❶ 去火车站怎么坐车？

Qù huǒchēzhàn zěnme zuò chē?

Which bus should I take to the railway station?

❷ 去飞机场怎么坐车？

Qù fēijīchǎng zěnme zuò chē?

Which bus should I take to the airport?

2. 买三张票，到阜成门。

Mǎi sān zhāng piào, dào Fùchéngmén.

I want to buy three tickets to Fuchengmen.

Nowadays, there are buses without conductors. You just need to put coins into the bus fare box. If you get on a regular bus, you need to buy a ticket from the conductor. All you need to do is to tell the conductor your destination and the number of tickets that you want to buy by saying: "Mǎi……piào, dào……" You can also use this sentence structure for buying train tickets and plane tickets. Here are more examples:

❶ 买两张票，到火车站。

Mǎi liǎng zhāng piào, dào huǒchēzhàn.

I want to buy two tickets to the railway station.

❷ 买一张票，到动物园的。

Mǎi yì zhāng piào, dào dòngwùyuán de.

I want to buy a ticket to the zoo.

练习
Exercises

一、读一读 Read the following words and phrases.

故宫	Gùgōng	the Forbidden City
长城	Chángchéng	the Great Wall
商场	shāngchǎng	department store
大厦	dàshà	plaza; large building
电影院	diànyǐngyuàn	cinema; movie theater
动物园	dòngwùyuán	zoo

公园	gōngyuán	park
体育馆	tǐyùguǎn	stadium
马路	mǎlù	street
天桥	tiānqiáo	overpass
地铁	dìtiě	subway
轻轨	qīngguǐ	light rail transit

二、试一试 Substitution drills.

1. 去<u>前门</u>怎么坐车?
   Qù <u>Qiánmén</u> zěnme zuò chē?

   动物园
   dòngwùyuán

   华联商场
   Huálián Shāngchǎng

   长安电影院
   Cháng'ān Diànyǐngyuàn

   京广大厦
   Jīngguǎng Dàshà

2. 买<u>三</u>张票,到<u>阜成门</u>。
   Mǎi <u>sān</u> zhāng piào, dào <u>Fùchéngmén</u>.

四 sì	工人体育馆 Gōngrén Tǐyùguǎn
三 sān	中山公园 Zhōngshān Gōngyuán
两 liǎng	北京站 Běijīng Zhàn
一 yì	西直门地铁站 Xīzhímén Dìtiězhàn

三、能力训练 Practice your Chinese.

1. 询问一个路人，从你所在的地方去乘地铁应该怎么走。

   Xúnwèn yí ge lùrén, cóng nǐ suǒ zài de dìfang qù chéng dìtiě yīnggāi zěnme zǒu.

   Ask a passer-by how to change to the subway station from where you are.

2. 你告诉售票员你要买一张票，到天安门。

   Nǐ gàosu shòupiàoyuán nǐ yào mǎi yì zhāng piào, dào Tiān'ān Mén.

   Tell the conductor you want to buy a ticket to Tian'anmen.

Lesson 17

发传真与寄快递
Fā Chuánzhēn Yǔ Jì Kuàidì
Sending a Fax or an Express Mail

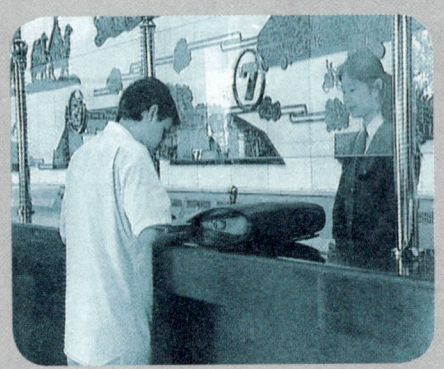

你知道吗?
Do you know?

Faxes can be sent and received at the business center of a hotel or in a professional shop. A domestic express mail in China takes about one or two days to reach the destination, while an international express mail takes longer, about three or four days. The EMS delivers various kinds of items, ranging from flowers and documents to food and electronic goods. Being quick and convenient, it is no doubt more expensive than ordinary mail service. To mail an express letter or parcel, you can go to a post office in person, or just call 11185 to ask for pick-up or home delivery service. Besides post offices, you can also have your goods or presents delivered by an express delivery company.

Sending a Fax or an Express Mail

生词
Vocabulary

❶ 发	fā	v.	send (a fax or an e-mail)
❷ 传真	chuánzhēn	n.	fax
❸ 文件	wénjiàn	n.	file; document
❹ 寄	jì	v.	post; send
❺ 特快专递	tèkuài zhuāndì	np.	EMS
❻ 联系	liánxì	v.	contact; get in touch with

句型
Sentence Patterns

❶ 我想往/给……发一份传真。
Wǒ xiǎng wǎng/gěi……fā yí fèn chuánzhēn.

❷ 寄到……的特快专递几天能到?
Jì dào……de tèkuài zhuāndì jǐ tiān néng dào?

情景会话
Situational Conversations

[Here is a man coming to the business center to send a fax.]

男 士:小姐,你们这里可以发传真吗?
Xiǎojiě, nǐmen zhèlǐ kěyǐ fā chuánzhēn ma?
Miss, can I send a fax here?

Lesson 17

服务员：可以。您要发到哪里?
Kěyǐ. Nín yào fā dào nǎli?
Yes. Where do you want to send it?

男　士：发一份国内传真多少钱?
Fā yí fèn guónèi chuánzhēn duōshao qián?
How much is the charge for a domestic fax?

服务员：一页纸10块钱。
Yí yè zhǐ shí kuài qián.
10 *yuan* a page.

男　士：我想往上海发一份传真。
Wǒ xiǎng wǎng Shànghǎi fā yí fèn chuánzhēn.
I want to send a fax to Shanghai.

服务员：请您把您的传真号码和文件给我。
Qǐng nín bǎ nín de chuánzhēn hàomǎ hé wénjiàn gěi wǒ.
Please give me the fax number and the document.

……

您的传真发完了。
Nín de chuánzhēn fāwán le.
Your fax has been transmitted.

男　士：谢谢。我应该付多少钱?
Xièxie. Wǒ yīnggāi fù duōshao qián?
Thank you. How much should I pay?

服务员：一共20块。
Yígòng èrshí kuài.
The total is 20 *yuan*.

Sending a Fax or an Express Mail

II

[Here is a student sending an EMS to Guangzhou.]

学生：小姐，我想寄一个特快专递到广州，几天能到？
Xiǎojiě, wǒ xiǎng jì yí ge tèkuài zhuāndì dào Guǎngzhōu, jǐ tiān néng dào?
Miss, I want to send an express mail to Guangzhou. How long does it take?

职员：一般三天。请把您的姓名、地址和联系电话写一下。
Yìbān sān tiān. Qǐng bǎ nín de xìngmíng、dìzhǐ hé liánxì diànhuà xiě yíxià.
Usually, it takes three days. Please write down your name, address and contact number.

常用表达法
Useful Phrases and Expressions

1. 我想往上海发一份传真。
Wǒ xiǎng wǎng Shànghǎi fā yí fèn chuánzhēn.
I want to send a fax to Shanghai.

Usually, you can make copies of your documents or send a fax at the business centers of a hotel. If you want to send a fax to someone or some place, you should say: "Wǒ xiǎng wǎng/gěi……fā yí fèn chuánzhēn." The following are more examples:

❶ 我想往美国发一份传真。
Wǒ xiǎng wǎng Měiguó fā yí fèn chuánzhēn.
I want to send a fax to the United States.

❷ 我想给我的父母发一份传真。
   Wǒ xiǎng gěi wǒ de fùmǔ fā yí fèn chuánzhēn.
   I want to send a fax to my parents.

2. 寄到广州的特快专递几天能到？
   Jì dào Guǎngzhōu de tèkuài zhuāndì jǐ tiān néng dào?
   How long does it take to send this to Guangzhou by EMS?

The EMS companies come to your door to deliver the service, and of course, you can go to the post office to use the EMS also. If you want to know how long it takes to send a parcel by EMS to somewhere, you may ask: "Jì dào……de tèkuài zhuāndì jǐ tiān néng dào?" Here are more examples:

❶ 寄到美国的特快专递几天能到？
   Jì dào Měiguó de tèkuài zhuāndì jǐ tiān néng dào?
   How long does it take to send this to the United States by EMS?

❷ 寄到日本的特快专递几天能到？
   Jì dào Rìběn de tèkuài zhuāndì jǐ tiān néng dào?
   How long does it take to send this to Japan by EMS?

练习
Exercises

一、读一读 Read the following words and phrases.

传真	chuánzhēn	fax; facsimile
电报	diànbào	telegram; cable
电子邮件	diànzǐ yóujiàn	e-mail
父母	fùmǔ	parents
亲戚	qīnqi	relative

Sending a Fax or an Express Mail

哥哥	gēge	elder brother
姐姐	jiějie	elder sister
弟弟	dìdi	younger brother
妹妹	mèimei	younger sister

二、试一试 Substitution drills.

1. 我想往上海发一份传真。
   Wǒ xiǎng wǎng Shànghǎi fā yí fèn chuánzhēn.

   往长城公司
   wǎng Chángchéng Gōngsī

   给我的朋友
   gěi wǒ de péngyou

   给在美国的父母
   gěi zài Měiguó de fùmǔ

   给北京大学留学生办公室
   gěi Běijīng Dàxué liúxuéshēng bàngōngshì

2. 寄到广州的特快专递几天能到?
   Jì dào Guǎngzhōu de tèkuài zhuāndì jǐ tiān néng dào?

   法国巴黎
   Fǎguó Bālí

   日本东京
   Rìběn Dōngjīng

   英国伦敦
   Yīngguó Lúndūn

   中国香港
   Zhōngguó Xiānggǎng

三、能力训练 Practice your Chinese.

1. 你要发一个传真给英国伦敦的朋友,询问一下附近哪里可以发传真,怎么收费。

   Nǐ yào fā yí ge chuánzhēn gěi Yīngguó Lúndūn de péngyou, xúnwèn yíxià fùjìn nǎli kěyǐ fā chuánzhēn, zěnme shōu fèi.

   You want to send a fax to a friend in London, UK. Ask where to send it and how much the charge is.

2. 你问服务员寄到上海的EMS几天能到。

   Nǐ wèn fúwùyuán jì dào Shànghǎi de EMS jǐ tiān néng dào.

   Ask an attendant how many days it will take for your EMS to reach Shanghai.

Lesson 18

在 邮 局
Zài Yóujú
At a Post Office

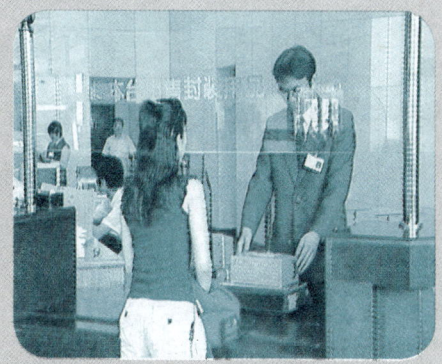

你知道吗?
Do you know?

With the development of high technology, people now more often keep in touch and communicate with each other via e-mail or telephone. Nevertheless, it would be a pleasure to receive a letter or postcard from afar. An ordinary airmail takes about one or two weeks to reach another country, while EMS takes only three days or so. All postal items going abroad are subject to customs inspection, so they can only be mailed in those big post offices with customs services.

生词
Vocabulary

❶	航空信	hángkōngxìn	np.	airmail
❷	挂号信	guàhàoxìn	np.	registered mail
❸	称	chēng	v.	weigh
❹	包裹	bāoguǒ	n.	parcel
❺	盒子	hézi	n.	box

句型
Sentence Patterns

❶ 我寄……信。
Wǒ jì……xìn.

❷ 我要寄……到……
Wǒ yào jì……dào……

情景会话
Situational Conversations

[Here is a customer mailing a letter.]

男　士：小姐，我想寄一封信到美国。
　　　　Xiǎojiě, wǒ xiǎng jì yì fēng xìn dào Měiguó.
　　　　Miss, I want to post a letter to the United States.

营业员：你寄航空信还是挂号信？
　　　　Nǐ jì hángkōngxìn háishi guàhàoxìn?
　　　　Do you want to post it by airmail or registered mail?

At a Post Office

男 士：我寄航空信。
　　　Wǒ jì hángkōngxìn.
　　　I want to post it by airmail.

营业员：请把信给我称一下。
　　　Qǐng bǎ xìn gěi wǒ chēng yíxià.
　　　Please give me the letter to weigh.

　　　……

　　　请贴5块4毛钱的邮票。
　　　Qǐng tiē wǔ kuài sì máo qián de yóupiào.
　　　Please affix five *yuan* and forty *fen* worth of stamps.

[Here is a customer mailing a parcel.]

女 士：先生，我要寄一个包裹到深圳。
　　　Xiānsheng, wǒ yào jì yí ge bāoguǒ dào Shēnzhèn.
　　　Sir, I'd like to mail a parcel to Shenzhen.

营业员：请先填一张包裹单。
　　　Qǐng xiān tián yì zhāng bāoguǒdān.
　　　Would you fill out a parcel form, please?

女 士：您看一下，这样填行吗？
　　　Nín kàn yíxià, zhèyàng tián xíng ma?
　　　Please have a look. Is it OK?

营业员：行。请您把要寄的东西给我看一下。
　　　Xíng. Qǐng nín bǎ yào jì de dōngxi gěi wǒ kàn yíxià.
　　　OK. Please show me what you are going to mail.

　　　……

您还需要买一个盒子。邮费和盒子一共是30块6毛。

Nín hái xūyào mǎi yí ge hézi. Yóufèi hé hézi yígòng shì sānshí kuài liù máo.

You also need to buy a cardboard box. The total cost for the postage and the cardboard box is thirty *yuan* and sixty *fen*.

女　士：请问几天能到？

Qǐngwèn jǐ tiān néng dào?

How long will it take?

营业员：一个星期吧。

Yí ge xīngqī ba.

About one week.

常用表达法

Useful Phrases and Expressions

1. 我寄航空信。

   Wǒ jì hángkōngxìn.

   I want to post it by airmail.

Mail includes ordinary mail—*pingxin*, registered mail—*guahaoxin* and airmail—*hangkongxin*. For ordinary domestic mail, you need to pay 120 *fen* for the stamp, and 80 *fen* for a local mail. If you want to send a very important letter, registered mail would be a good choice. At the post office, if you are asked what kind of mail service you prefer, you can say: "Wǒ jì……xìn." The following are more examples:

❶ 我寄挂号信。

   Wǒ jì guàhàoxìn.

   I'll post it by registered mail.

At a Post Office

❷ 我寄平信。
Wǒ jì píngxìn.
I'll post it by ordinary mail.

2. 我要寄一个包裹到深圳。
Wǒ yào jì yí ge bāoguǒ dào Shēnzhèn.
I would like to mail a parcel to Shenzhen.

When mailing a parcel at the post office, you have to use a standard-sized box provided by the post office. A check-up on the parcel is a routine before the box is sealed. When mailing something, you need to say: "Wǒ yào jì……dào……" Here are more examples:

❶ 我要寄一个包裹到美国。
Wǒ yào jì yí ge bāoguǒ dào Měiguó.
I would like to mail a parcel to the United States.

❷ 我要寄一些衣服到北京。
Wǒ yào jì yìxiē yīfu dào Běijīng.
I would like to mail some clothes to Beijing.

练习
Exercises

一、读一读 Read the following words and phrases.

一封平信	yì fēng píngxìn	an ordinary mail
一封挂号信	yì fēng guàhàoxìn	a registered mail
一封航空信	yì fēng hángkōngxìn	an airmail
一个特快专递	yí ge tèkuài zhuāndì	an express mail
一张明信片	yì zhāng míngxìnpiàn	a postcard
一张贺年卡	yì zhāng hèniánkǎ	a New Year card

一个包裹	yí ge bāoguǒ	a parcel
一些东西	yìxiē dōngxi	some stuff
一些衣服	yìxiē yīfu	some clothes
几张照片	jǐ zhāng zhàopiàn	some photographs

二、**试一试** Substitution drills.

1. 我寄<u>一封航空信</u>。
   Wǒ jì yì fēng hángkōngxìn.

   > 两封平信
   > liǎng fēng píngxìn
   >
   > 一封挂号信
   > yì fēng guàhàoxin
   >
   > 几张明信片
   > jǐ zhāng míngxìnpiàn
   >
   > 一个包裹
   > yí ge bāoguǒ

2. 我要寄<u>一个包裹</u>到<u>深圳</u>。
   Wǒ yào jì yí ge bāoguǒ dào Shēnzhèn.

   > 一些衣服   法国
   > yìxiē yīfu   Fǎguó
   >
   > 一个特快专递   南京
   > yí ge tèkuài zhuāndì   Nánjīng
   >
   > 一封航空信   东京
   > yì fēng hángkōngxìn   Dōngjīng
   >
   > 十张贺年卡   香港
   > shí zhāng hèniánkǎ   Xiānggǎng

三、能力训练 Practice your Chinese.

1. 普通信件叫什么？在你们那儿，寄一封市内普通信件多少钱？挂号信呢？

   Pǔtōng xìnjiàn jiào shénme? Zài nǐmen nàr, jì yì fēng shìnèi pǔtōng xìnjiàn duōshao qián? Guàhàoxìn ne?

   What is Chinese for "ordinary mail"? What's the charge for posting an ordinary mail within the city where you are? What about posting a registered mail?

2. 你告诉邮局工作人员你要寄一个包裹到香港。

   Nǐ gàosu yóujú gōngzuò rényuán nǐ yào jì yí ge bāoguǒ dào Xiānggǎng.

   Tell the attendant in the post office that you want to mail a parcel to Hong Kong.

Lesson 19

点菜 I
Diǎn Cài I
Ordering Dishes (I)

Do you know?

Chinese people like dining together with lots of friends. Unlike in the West where everyone eats food in his/her own plate, in China, either eating at home or in a restaurant, it is customary to put all the dishes together for people to share. There are 8 major styles of Chinese cuisines. Generally speaking, the southerners prefer rice, while the northerners like wheaten food better. Rice, noodles and other staple food are not served at the same time with the dishes. Usually drinks come first, then the dishes, and the staple food will be served at last according to the needs of guests. No dessert is served after the meal, though some restaurants do provide fruits when a meal comes to the end.

Ordering Dishes (Ⅰ)

生词
Vocabulary

❶	菜单	càidān	n.	menu
❷	点菜	diǎn cài	vp.	order dishes
❸	宫保鸡丁	Gōngbǎo Jīdīng	pn.	Kung Pao Chicken
❹	烧茄子	Shāo Qiézi	pn.	Braised Eggplants
❺	糖醋排骨	Táng-cù Páigǔ	pn.	Sweet and Sour Spare Ribs
❻	古老肉	Gǔlǎoròu	pn.	Sweet and Sour Pork

句型
Sentence Patterns

❶ 来一个……
Lái yí ge……

❷ 你可以给我们介绍几个……菜吗?
Nǐ kěyǐ gěi wǒmen jièshào jǐ ge……cài ma?

情景会话
Situational Conversations

Ⅰ

[Here are two persons ordering dishes.]

男　士：小姐，拿菜单来。
　　　　Xiǎojiě, ná càidān lái.
　　　　Miss, let me see the menu.

服务员：你们好。你们可以点菜了吗？

Nǐmen hǎo. Nǐmen kěyǐ diǎn cài le ma?

Hello, are you ready to order now?

男　士：来一个宫保鸡丁、一个烧茄子、一个鸡蛋汤，再要两碗米饭、一个炒饭。

Lái yí ge Gōngbǎo Jīdīng, yí ge Shāo Qiézi, yí ge Jīdàn Tāng, zài yào liǎng wǎn mǐfàn, yí ge chǎofàn.

We would like Kung Pao Chicken, Braised Eggplants, Egg Drop Soup, two bowls of rice and a plate of fried rice.

II

[Here are some foreign students ordering food.]

留学生：小姐，我们是第一次到中国来，你可以给我们介绍几个好吃的中国菜吗？

Xiǎojiě, wǒmen shì dì-yī cì dào Zhōngguó lái, nǐ kěyǐ gěi wǒmen jièshào jǐ ge hǎochī de Zhōngguó cài ma?

Miss, this is our first time to China. Could you recommend some delicious dishes to us?

服务员：当然可以。我们这里的宫保鸡丁、糖醋排骨、古老肉和烧茄子都很有名。

Dāngrán kěyǐ. Wǒmen zhèli de Gōngbǎo Jīdīng、Táng-cù Páigǔ、Gǔlǎoròu hé Shāo Qiézi dōu hěn yǒumíng.

Certainly. Our Kung Pao Chicken, Sweet and Sour Spare Ribs, Sweet and Sour Pork and Braised Eggplants are very famous.

留学生：那我们每种要一个，再来三碗米饭。

Nà wǒmen měi zhǒng yào yí ge, zài lái sān wǎn mǐfàn.

Well, then we'd like one of each of those, and three bowls of rice.

服务员：好，请稍等。

Hǎo, qǐng shāo děng.

OK. Wait a moment, please.

常用表达法
Useful Phrases and Expressions

1. 来一个宫保鸡丁、一个鸡蛋汤和一碗米饭。
   Lái yí ge Gōngbǎo Jīdīng、yí ge Jīdàn Tāng hé yì wǎn mǐfàn.
   We would like Kung Pao Chicken, Egg Drop Soup and a bowl of rice.

Kung Pao Chicken, Braised Eggplants, Sweet and Sour Spare Ribs, Sweet and Sour Pork are some of the popular Chinese dishes among foreign visitors. Next time, try some of these at a Chinese restaurant. If you know quite a bit about Chinese cuisine, and you know what you want to eat, you can just order the food by saying: "Lái yí ge……" The following are more examples:

❶ 来一个炒饭和一个酸辣汤。
   Lái yí ge chǎofàn hé yí ge Suān-là Tāng.
   I would like Fried Rice and Sour and Spicy Soup.

❷ 来两碗面条和一瓶啤酒。
   Lái liǎng wǎn miàntiáo hé yì píng píjiǔ.
   I want two bowls of noodles and a bottle of beer.

2. 你可以给我们介绍几个好吃的菜吗？
   Nǐ kěyǐ gěi wǒmen jièshào jǐ ge hǎochī de cài ma?
   Could you recommend some delicious dishes to us?

If you know very little about Chinese food, you can ask the waiter/waitress for assistance. You can say: "Nǐ kěyǐ gěi wǒmen jièshào jǐ ge……cài ma?" Here are more examples:

❶ 你可以给我们介绍几个特色菜吗?
Nǐ kěyǐ gěi wǒmen jièshào jǐ ge tèsè cài ma?
Could you recommend some specialties to us?

❷ 你可以给我们介绍几个凉菜吗?
Nǐ kěyǐ gěi wǒmen jièshào jǐ ge liángcài ma?
Could you recommend some cold dishes to us?

练习
Exercises

一、读一读 Read the following words and phrases.

米饭	mǐfàn	rice
面条	miàntiáo	noodles
馒头	mántou	steamed bun; steamed bread
包子	bāozi	steamed stuffed bun
饺子	jiǎozi	dumpling (with meat and vegetable stuffing)
炒饭	chǎofàn	fried rice
鸡蛋汤	Jīdàn Tāng	Egg Drop Soup
豆腐汤	Dòufu Tāng	Tofu Soup
鱼汤	Yú Tāng	Fish Soup
酸辣汤	Suān-là Tāng	Sour and Spicy Soup
一瓶矿泉水	yì píng kuàngquánshuǐ	a bottle of mineral water
一壶茶	yì hú chá	a pot of tea
一碗粥	yì wǎn zhōu	a bowl of porridge
一双筷子	yì shuāng kuàizi	a pair of chopsticks
一副刀叉	yí fù dāo-chā	a pair of knife and fork

Ordering Dishes (Ⅰ)

二、试一试 Substitution drills.

1. 来<u>一个宫保鸡丁、一个鸡蛋汤和一碗米饭</u>。
   Lái yí ge Gōngbǎo Jīdīng、yí ge Jīdàn Tāng hé yì wǎn mǐfàn.

   > 两个包子和一碗酸辣汤
   > liǎng ge bāozi hé yì wǎn Suān-là Tāng
   >
   > 一碗面条和一个糖醋排骨
   > yì wǎn miàntiáo hé yí ge Táng-cù Páigǔ
   >
   > 一个炒饭和一碗鸡蛋汤
   > yí ge chǎofàn hé yì wǎn Jīdàn Tāng
   >
   > 一斤饺子、两瓶啤酒
   > yì jīn jiǎozi、liǎng píng píjiǔ

2. 你可以给我们介绍几个<u>好吃的中国菜</u>吗?
   Nǐ kěyǐ gěi wǒmen jièshào jǐ ge <u>hǎochī de Zhōngguócài</u> ma?

   > 不辣的菜
   > bú là de cài
   >
   > 这里的特色菜
   > zhèli de tèsècài
   >
   > 汤
   > tāng
   >
   > 用豆腐做的菜
   > yòng dòufu zuò de cài

三、能力训练 Practice your Chinese.

1. 你知道哪些中国菜的名字?请说一说。
   Nǐ zhīdào nǎxiē Zhōngguócài de míngzi? Qǐng shuō yi shuō.
   Say the names of the Chinese dishes you know.

2. 到中国餐馆向服务员要一份菜单,了解一下这个饭馆有哪些特色菜,并试着点菜。

Dào Zhōngguó cānguǎn xiàng fúwùyuán yào yí fèn càidān, liǎojiě yíxià zhège fànguǎn yǒu nǎxiē tèsè cài, bìng shìzhe diǎn cài.

Ask the waiter/waitress for a menu at a Chinese restaurant to see what its specialties are, and try to order some dishes.

点 菜 II
Diǎn Cài II
Ordering Dishes (II)

Do you know?

    As the old saying goes, every man has his hobbyhorse. When ordering a dish, you may follow your own taste and ask the chef to do some minor adaptations to the recipe, such as adding or reducing certain ingredients. Chefs are fully capable of making some innovations and improvements to cater to the tastes of customers.

127

生词
Vocabulary

❶	咸	xián	*adj.*	salty
❷	盐	yán	*n.*	salt
❸	厨师	chúshī	*n.*	cook; chef
❹	辣椒	làjiāo	*n.*	hot pepper; chilli
❺	葱	cōng	*n.*	scallion; Chinese onion
❻	姜	jiāng	*n.*	ginger
❼	蒜	suàn	*n.*	garlic

句型
Sentence Patterns

❶ (上次)你们的菜太……了,(这次)……
   (Shàng cì) nǐmen de cài tài……le, (zhè cì)……

❷ ……里别放……
   ……lǐ bié fàng……

情景会话
Situational Conversations

[Here are two people having a meal together.]

男 士:我们要一个宫保鸡丁,一个鸡蛋汤。
      Wǒmen yào yí ge Gōngbǎo Jīdīng, yí ge Jīdàn Tāng.
      We would like to have Kung Pao Chicken and Egg Drop Soup.

Ordering Dishes (II)

女　士：小姐，上次我在这儿吃饭，菜做得太咸了，这次少放些盐。

Xiǎojiě, shàng cì wǒ zài zhèr chī fàn, cài zuò de tài xián le, zhè cì shǎo fàng xiē yán.

Miss, last time I had my meal here and the dishes were too salty. Please put less salt in this time.

服务员：好，我会告诉厨师的。

Hǎo, wǒ huì gàosu chúshī de.

OK, I will tell it to the chef.

男　士：我们要一个辣子鸡，好不好？

Wǒmen yào yí ge Làzi Jī, hǎo bu hǎo?

Shall we have Sautéed Diced Chicken with Chili and Pepper?

女　士：我不能吃辣的。

Wǒ bù néng chī là de.

I can't eat spicy food.

男　士：那让厨师少放点儿辣椒。

Nà ràng chúshī shǎo fàng diǎnr làjiāo.

Well, we can ask the cook to use less hot pepper.

女　士：汤里别放葱、姜、蒜。

Tāng li bié fàng cōng、jiāng、suàn.

Oh yes, don't put scallion, ginger or garlic in the soup.

服务员：我记下来了。还有别的要求吗？

Wǒ jì xiàlai le. Hái yǒu biéde yāoqiú ma?

I have written your orders down. Anything else?

女　士：没有了。请快点儿。

Méiyǒu le. Qǐng kuài diǎnr.

Nothing else. Please be quick.

服务员：好，请稍等。

Hǎo, qǐng shāo děng.

All right. Wait a moment, please.

常用表达法
Useful Phrases and Expressions

1. 上次的菜做得太咸了，这次少放些盐。
   Shàng cì de cài zuò de tài xián le, zhè cì shǎo fàng xiē yán.
   Last time the dishes were too salty. Please put less salt in this time.

When having a meal with friends at a restaurant where you have previously eaten, you may not want to have food again that you didn't like the first time. To do this, you just have to speak up and tell the waiter/waitress what you want the dishes to be like by saying: "……de cài zuò de tài……le, ……" The following are more examples:

❶ 昨天的菜做得太甜了，今天少放点儿糖。
   Zuótiān de cài zuò de tài tián le, jīntiān shǎo fàng diǎnr táng.
   Your dishes yesterday were too sweet. Please use less sugar today.

❷ 上次的菜做得太辣了，这次少放点儿辣椒。
   Shàng cì de cài zuò de tài là le, zhè cì shǎo fàng diǎnr làjiāo.
   Your dishes last time were too hot. Put less hot pepper in this time, please.

2. 汤里别放葱、姜、蒜。
   Tāng li bié fàng cōng、jiāng、suàn.
   Don't put scallion, ginger or garlic in the soup.

Ordering Dishes (II)

You can also ask the chef to prepare the dishes exactly to your taste. For example, many people do not like scallion, ginger, garlic, hot pepper or some other seasonings in their foods. You can tell the chef by saying: "……li bié fàng……." Here are more examples:

❶ 菜里别放味精。
   Cài li bié fàng wèijīng.
   Don't put MSG in the dishes.

❷ 菜里别放辣椒。
   Cài li bié fàng làjiāo.
   Don't put hot pepper in the dishes.

练习
Exercises

一、读一读 Read the following words and phrases.

甜	tián	sweet
酸	suān	sour
苦	kǔ	bitter
辣	là	hot
咸	xián	salty
淡	dàn	tasteless; light
鲜	xiān	delicious; tasty
（油）腻	(yóu)nì	(of food) greasy; oily
葱	cōng	scallion; Chinese onion
姜	jiāng	ginger
蒜	suàn	garlic
香菜	xiāngcài	caraway
辣椒	làjiāo	hot pepper; chilli
胡椒面	hújiāomiàn	ground pepper
咖喱	gālí	curry

糖	táng	sugar
盐	yán	salt
醋	cù	vinegar
酱油	jiàngyóu	soy sauce
香油	xiāngyóu	sesame oil
味精	wèijīng	monosodium glutamate (MSG)

二、试一试 Substitution drills.

1. 上次你们的<u>菜</u>做得太咸了，这次<u>少放些盐</u>。
   Shàng cì nǐmen de <u>cài</u> zuò de tài xián le, zhè cì <u>shǎo fàng xiē yán</u>.

汤 tāng	辣 là	少放些胡椒面 shǎo fàng xiē hújiāomiàn
菜 cài	淡 dàn	多放点儿盐 duō fàng diǎnr yán
糖醋排骨 Táng-cù Páigǔ	甜 tián	少放些糖 shǎo fàng xiē táng
包子 bāozi	腻 nì	少放些肉 shǎo fàng xiē ròu

2. <u>汤</u>里别放<u>葱、姜、蒜</u>。
   <u>Tāng</u> li bié fàng <u>cōng、jiāng、suàn</u>.

菜 Cài	味精 wèijīng
菜 Cài	醋和酱油 cù hé jiàngyóu
饺子 Jiǎozi	葱和姜 cōng hé jiāng
面条 Miàntiáo	辣椒 làjiāo

三、能力训练 Practice your Chinese.

1. 点菜时你告诉服务员，你不喜欢吃辣椒，另外菊花茶里别加糖。

   Diǎn cài shí nǐ gàosu fúwùyuán, nǐ bù xǐhuan chī làjiāo, lìngwài júhuāchá li bié jiā táng.

   Tell the waiter/waitress when you order your dishes that you do not like hot peppers and not to put sugar in chrysanthemum tea.

2. 你要求服务员菜和汤里都不要放味精。

   Nǐ yāoqiú fúwùyuán cài hé tāng li dōu bú yào fàng wèijīng.

   Ask him/her not to put any MSG in your dishes and soup.

词语索引
Index of Words and Phrases

Lesson	Chinese	*Pinyin*	Grammar Terms	English
12	办公室	bàngōngshì	n.	office
18	包裹	bāoguǒ	n.	parcel
7	标准间	biāozhǔnjiān	np.	standard room
4	表	biǎo	n.	meter
19	菜单	càidān	n.	menu
10	参加	cānjiā	v.	take part in
3	厕所	cèsuǒ	n.	toilet
5	钞票	chāopiào	n.	bill; bank note
18	称	chēng	v.	weigh
4	出口	chūkǒu	n.	exit
10	出去	chūqu	v.	go out
20	厨师	chúshī	n.	cook; chef
17	传真	chuánzhēn	n.	fax
20	葱	cōng	n.	scallion; Chinese onion
7	单人间	dānrénjiān	np.	single room
9	灯	dēng	n.	light
16	地铁	dìtiě	n.	subway
19	点菜	diǎn cài	vp.	order dishes
14	电话费	diànhuàfèi	np.	telephone charge
16	动物园	dòngwùyuán	n.	zoo
9	堵	dǔ	v.	block up (of toilets of kitchen)
6	度	dù	m.	degree

6	多云	duōyún	n.	cloudy
17	发	fā	v.	send (a fax or an e-mail)
4	发票	fāpiào	n.	bill; receipt
8	房卡	fángkǎ	n.	room card
10	分机	fēnjī	n.	extension
3	附近	fùjìn	n.	nearby
4	高速公路	gāosù gōnglù	np.	expressway
19	宫保鸡丁	Gōngbǎo Jīdīng	pn.	Kung Pao Chicken
19	古老肉	Gǔlǎoròu	pn.	Sweet and Sour Pork
18	挂号信	guàhàoxìn	np.	registered mail
4	拐	guǎi	v.	make a turn
16	过	guò	v.	pass; cross
16	过街天桥	guòjiē tiānqiáo	np.	overhead pedestrian crossing
1	海关	hǎiguān	n.	customs
2	航班	hángbān	n.	airline flight; scheduled flight
18	航空信	hángkōngxìn	np.	airmail
18	盒子	hézi	n.	box
1	护照	hùzhào	n.	passport
5	换	huàn	v.	exchange
16	换(车)	huàn (chē)	v.	transfer buses (trains)
17	寄	jì	v.	post; send
13	加急	jiājí	adj.	urgent
15	检票	jiǎn piào	v.	punch a ticket
20	姜	jiāng	n.	ginger

8	结账	jié zhàng	v.	settle the bill
10	聚会	jùhuì	n.	get-together; party
7	空	kōng	adj.	vacant
10	空儿	kòngr	n.	free; free time
11	口信	kǒuxìn	n.	oral message
20	辣椒	làjiāo	n.	hot pepper; chilli
15	劳驾	láo jià	v.	excuse me
17	联系	liánxì	v.	contact; get in touch with
15	列车	lièchē	n.	train
3	楼梯	lóutī	n.	stairs; stairway
3	麻烦	máfan	n./v.	trouble/bother
13	毛料	máoliào	n.	woolen
5	面值	miànzhí	n.	denomination
13	内衣	nèiyī	n.	underclothes
14	哦	ò	int.	Oh (indicating understanding or realization)
9	派	pài	v.	send; dispatch
6	气温	qìwēn	n.	air temperature; atmospheric temperature
5	签名	qiān míng	v.	sign one's name
12	前天	qiántiān	n.	the day before yesterday
11	亲戚	qīnqi	n.	relatives
6	晴	qíng	adj.	fine; clear
2	取	qǔ	v.	take; get; fetch
1	入境	rù jìng	v.	enter the customs

19	烧茄子	Shāo Qiézi	pn.	Braised Eggplants
1	生意	shēngyi	n.	business
15	十字路口	shízì lùkǒu	np.	intersection
14	收银台	shōuyíntái	np.	cashier desk
1	手续	shǒuxù	n.	procedures; formalities
5	数	shǔ	v.	count (money)
20	蒜	suàn	n.	garlic
14	算	suàn	v.	calculate
19	糖醋排骨	Táng-cù Páigǔ	pn.	Sweet and Sour Spare Ribs
7	套间	tàojiān	n.	suite
17	特快专递	tèkuài zhuāndì	np.	EMS
6	天气	tiānqì	n.	weather
8	填	tián	v.	fill in
8	退房	tuì fáng	vp.	check out of the hotel
17	文件	wénjiàn	n.	file; document
6	雾	wù	n.	fog
13	西装	xīzhuāng	n.	Western suit
3	洗手间	xǐshǒujiān	n.	toilet; restroom
9	下水道	xiàshuǐdào	n.	drain; sewer
20	咸	xián	adj.	salty
2	行李	xíngli	n.	luggage; baggage
2	行李车	xínglichē	np.	luggage cart
2	行李带	xínglidài	np.	conveyor belt
9	修	xiū	v.	repair; fix
8	押金	yājīn	n.	deposit
20	盐	yán	n.	salt

6	阴	yīn	adj.	overcast
13	油迹	yóujì	n.	oil stain
6	雨夹雪	yǔ jiā xuě	np.	rain and snow
6	预报	yùbào	v.	forecast
7	预订	yùdìng	v.	reserve; make a reservation
12	预约	yùyuē	v.	make an appointment
8	钥匙	yàoshi	n.	key
15	站	zhàn	n.	station; stop
15	站台	zhàntái	n.	platform (in a railway station)
14	账单	zhàngdān	n.	bill
5	支票	zhīpiào	n.	check (cheque)
8	住房登记卡	zhùfáng dēngjìkǎ	np.	registration form
6	转	zhuǎn	v.	turn; shift; change
11	转告	zhuǎngào	v.	pass on a message (to a person)
9	租	zū	v.	rent